C000132227

HAUNTED
ST ANDREWS

HAUNTED ST ANDREWS

Geoff Holder

The
History
Press

To all the tribe of SADIML.

First published 2012

The History Press
The Mill, Brimscombe Port
Stroud, Gloucestershire, GL5 2QG
www.thehistorypress.co.uk

© Geoff Holder, 2012

The right of Geoff Holder to be identified as the Author
of this work has been asserted in accordance with the
Copyrights, Designs and Patents Act 1988.

All rights reserved. No part of this book may be reprinted
or reproduced or utilised in any form or by any electronic,
mechanical or other means, now known or hereafter invented,
including photocopying and recording, or in any information
storage or retrieval system, without the permission in writing
from the Publishers.

British Library Cataloguing in Publication Data.
A catalogue record for this book is available from the British Library.

ISBN 978 0 7524 5848 9
Typesetting and origination by The History Press
Printed in Great Britain

Contents

Acknowledgements

BLESSINGS to; the library angels of St Andrews Public Library, the Special Collections Unit of the Library of the University of St Andrews, Kirkcaldy Central Library, and the Local Studies Section of the A.K. Bell Library in Perth. For assistance, thanks to David Orr and Alan Tricker of the Byre Theatre, Amy Dale of the Museums Collections Unit, and Lorn Macintyre. Special thanks to Basia Rostworowska and Paul Kienewicz for adding a new twist to the story of the Pitmilly Poltergeist. Extra special thanks to Ségolène Dupuy and Jamie Cook.

This book is part of a series of works by Geoff Holder for The History Press, dedicated to the mysterious and paranormal. For more information, or to contribute your own experience, please visit www.geoffholder.com.

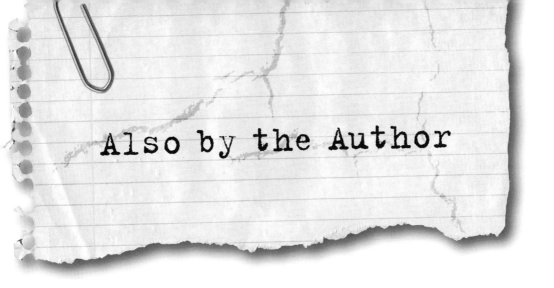

Also by the Author

Bloody British History: Edinburgh
Haunted Aberdeen & District
Haunted Dundee
The Little Book of Glasgow
Paranormal Cumbria
Paranormal Dundee
Paranormal Glasgow
Paranormal Perthshire
Scottish Bodysnatchers: A Gazetteer
The Guide to Mysterious Aberdeen
The Guide to Mysterious Aberdeenshire
The Guide to Mysterious Arran
The Guide to Mysterious Glasgow
The Guide to Mysterious Iona and Staffa
The Guide to the Mysterious Lake District
The Guide to Mysterious Loch Ness
The Guide to Mysterious Perthshire
The Guide to Mysterious Skye and Lochalsh
The Guide to Mysterious Stirlingshire
101 Things to Do with a Stone Circle

Introduction

We come to…the decayed city of
St. Andrews (which may also be styled a
Gothic Pompeii from the number of its ruins).
Handbook for Travellers in Scotland, 1875

ANY book about haunted St Andrews owes a great debt to *St Andrews Ghost Stories*, a small volume first published in 1911 and still in print. The author, William T. Linskill, was a major force in St Andrews for decades, serving on the town council under the title of Dean of Guild, exporting the game of golf to his *alma mater,* Cambridge University, and encouraging the 'howkings' – diggings for the underground tunnels and chambers that he believed ran beneath the medieval ruins of the cathedral area.

Unfortunately, any serious book about haunted St Andrews also has to acknowledge that *St Andrews Ghost Stories* is a farrago of fiction, fancy and folklore, mixed up with the odd bit of fact. Despite his famously bluff manner, Linskill was a dyed-in-the-wool romantic who wanted above all else to see a ghost. He never got his wish, and his book betrays the powerful influences of the fictions of M.R. James

and Charles Dickens, as well as a host of Gothic novels, plus several legends borrowed directly from elsewhere. All of which is a bit of a shame, because, when the urge took him, Linskill could worry away at historical mysteries like a terrier, and his input into the story of the Haunted Tower (*see* Chapter 1) has been invaluable.

Linskill died in 1929. The same year, H.V. Morton included an interview with the seventy-four-year-old in his travel book *In Search of Scotland*. Describing the ghost-hunter as looking like 'a possibly violent retired major-general', Morton found Linskill combative, sharp-minded and larger-than-life. Linskill related how, in his

St Andrews in 1693. The ruined cathedral and the monastic precinct are centre-right, with the tower of St Salvator's situated in the centre. (From John Slezar's Theatrum Scotiae*)*

Looking west towards St Salvator's along North Street, sometime before the First World War. (Author's Collection)

search for the supernatural, he had spent a night in the Haunted Tower with a bottle of whisky, and had attended numerous séances, all of which came to naught – in fact, at sittings with mediums he was 'cast out' from the circle of sitters because he was an 'unbeliever' and a 'sceptic'. I consider it a great pity that the astringent attitude he displayed in real life did not come to the fore when compiling the contents of *St Andrews Ghost Stories*. That being said, if you hunger for tales of yesteryear in which impatient toffs say things like, 'Zounds, Sir!' and 'Gadzooks, and oddbodkins, Sir!' then it's very much the book for you.

St Andrews Ghost Stories has two kinds of ghost story. The first are ludicrously over-the-top Gothic fripperies, in which the upper-class narrators all have short, sensible names while the 'rude mechanicals' of the amusing working-classes labour through life bearing the weight of names such as: Jeremiah and Concrikketty Anklebone, Messrs Snaggers and Darkgood, Maria Trombone, Jemima Podge, Teresa Shadbolt and Pellingham Truffles. The second consist of Linskill's interviews with anonymous informants whose experiences may actually have been rooted in the real world. These episodes, which form a minority

report within the book as a whole, are the most interesting parts of *St Andrews Ghost Stories*, and are referred to in the chapters that follow.

As for *Haunted St Andrews*, Chapter 1 deals with St Andrews' most famous ghost (the White Lady) and its most famous paranormal location (the Haunted Tower); it is my contention that I may have solved at least part of the mystery of the mummified body in the tower. Chapter 2 explores the numerous ghosts – historical and contemporary – that appear to cluster around the medieval quarter of the Pends and St Leonard's. Chapters 3 and 4 catalogue ghosts reported from the cathedral, the university, the castle and the old town. Chapters 5 and 6 get involved with a trio of poltergeists – including one that resulted in an insurance pay-out – while Chapter 7 rounds off with some apparitions betokening death, an encounter with an evil vortex on a beach, and a truly extraordinary vision of a phantom village.

My personal bugbear is books on the supernatural that lack anything in the way of a critical apparatus, where the reader is unable to check references or see where the writer obtained the information. For this reason, all the stories in *Haunted*

St Andrews from the top of St Rule's Tower. In the background, the haar is rolling in. (Photo by Geoff Holder)

St Andrews shrouded in thick fog. (Photo by Geoff Holder)

St Andrews are referred back to their original source, whether this be a newspaper, an ancient book, or an online chat-room. This, combined with the Bibliography at the end of the book, should enable you to determine whether I have been both fair and accurate, and whether you agree with my interpretations.

St Andrews is a small burgh characterised by an immense catalogue of antiquity; the cathedral, castle and university buildings dominate the town architecturally, while the medieval street plan is still evident in the way North Street, Market Street and South Street, radiate east from the cathedral, with interconnecting north-south lanes and wynds running between them. St Andrews is also sited on the very tip of the Fife coast, which means not only plentiful gobbets of wind and rain, but also the *haar* – the thick sea-fog that rolls in from the North Sea. When the haar seeps into the cobbled lanes, ancient buildings, the gaunt ruins and the old-world town, they all take on a distinct character redolent of centuries gone by. In the fog, the streetlights glow like gas lamps. Sounds are muffled. Sharp edges become hazy. Arched ruins loom out of the edge of vision. You almost expect a horse-drawn Victorian carriage to clatter out of the gloom.

Now, in many ways, I distrust a place that has 'atmosphere', because it gets in the way of investigation. The imagination takes over and we see and feel – or *think* we see and feel – evidence of the supernatural, when this may just be our emotional tendency to prefer the crepuscular to the unspectacular. But once wrapped in its mantle of luminous fog, the ancient fabric of St Andrews becomes a half-world, of things half-seen and half-feared, an environment of anxiety and anticipation; a place where ghosts might indeed walk.

Zounds, Sir!

Geoff Holder, 2012

1

The White Lady and the Haunted Tower

Go forth and win the haunted tower!

Andrew Lang, 'The Haunted Tower', 1889-90

THE 'White Lady' is without doubt the most written-about ghost of St Andrews, and her link with the so-called 'Haunted Tower' makes her story all the more fascinating, for here lies a murky story not just of the spirit of an attractive young woman, but of mummified bodies and corpse-stealing. The entire subject is garnered with a heavy sprinkling of myth-making, factual confusion, claims and counterclaims, all leavened by a dose of fictional invention and obfuscation. It's time to sort the wheat from the White Lady chaff.

There are two separate factors to the tale – the apparition of the White Lady herself, and what exactly was discovered in the vaults of what became known as the Haunted Tower. We do not know how far back sightings of the former go, nor do we have any clear idea when the structure in the precinct wall of the cathedral became known as the Haunted Tower. By the time people started writing about the subject in the 1860s, both elements were

well-established features in the ghost lore of St Andrews.

William Linskill provides us with both the most fantastical exploits of the White Lady, and, in contrast, a more sober documentary record. The former come, as expected, from *St Andrews Ghost Stories*, while the latter can be found in *The Strange Story of St Andrews Haunted Tower,* a now-obscure pamphlet reprinting an article he wrote originally for the *St Andrews Citizen* in 1925.

The Setting

The Haunted Tower is the rectangular two-storey structure in the imposing precinct wall, immediately north of the shattered west gable of the cathedral. The cathedral and priory were enclosed by a wall from at least the 1300s, although the current wall dates from the early fifteenth century, having been built during the priorate of John Hepburn (?-1522). Rising up to twenty feet high, enclosing an area of some thirty acres, and running almost a mile in length, the great wall, still substantially complete, is one of the marvels of medieval

The Haunted Tower and the cathedral graveyard. (Photo by Geoff Holder)

The Haunted Tower today. The steps lead up to the chamber where the bodies were found in 1868. (Photo by Geoff Holder)

Scotland. It was fortified by sixteen wall-towers, of which thirteen remain. The Haunted Tower is unusual in being rectangular rather than round, and consists of two rooms: a vault below the present ground level, and a kind of L-shaped watchroom on the first floor, reached by a short external stair. This upper chamber has a maximum length of ten feet, eight inches. There are gun loops and, on the outside face, two niches that probably held statues of the Blessed Virgin Mary. Alongside these niches is an armorial panel carved with the arms of Prior Hepburn, and a pot of lilies representing the Virgin. There was once a parapet walkway running along the top of the wall and passing through the upper part of the tower, although this has long collapsed.

At some unknown date, but obviously after the Reformation of 1560, when the cathedral was effectively abandoned, the two rooms of the tower were taken over by someone with money and influence, and converted into a kind of family mausoleum. When the ruins were returned to state care in 1826, both chambers had been sealed up since time immemorial, keeping their secret cargo of corpses to themselves. Over the next few decades, the cathedral ruins were stripped of the accumulated debris and soil of centuries, and slowly took on the visitor-friendly form we see today. Captain Daniel Wilson, who was born in 1844, told Linskill that, as a boy, he and his several brothers had the job of assisting their father with his work on the shipping beacon that once stood on one of the neighbouring towers. After lighting or extinguishing the beacon, the young lads, bold as day, would climb the ivy that then festooned the precinct wall – stealing birds' nests and eggs. During these expeditions they would bravely peer through the chinks in the masonry of the tower, gazing in awe and terror at what appeared to be the preserved corpse of a lovely young woman, lying in a coffin from which the lid had fallen off. If this reminiscence is accurate – Wilson was remembering back from his old age in the 1920s – then we can assume that the secret of the tower was starting to become known by the 1850s, and it may be from this time that we can date stories of the townsfolk (especially the fisher families) starting to avoid the tower after dark, always rushing past it fearfully as they walked around the outside of the wall on Kirkhill. The sealed rectangular structure was now, very definitely, the Haunted Tower.

The barred gate of the upper chamber – the site of the mysterious mummies. (Photo by Geoff Holder)

The Discovery of the Mummies

How the corpses in the tower came to be formally discovered is a matter of some dispute – and a great deal of overlapping claims. However, if we can trust the accumulated recollections of those involved, gathered by Linskill for the *Haunted Tower* pamphlet – plus a few others taken from contemporary newspapers – then the tower was entered at least four times in the nineteenth century. The first time appears to have been in early 1868. I date it thus because the only named witness was the Revd Skinner, who, in 1867, became the first priest of the new St Andrew's Episcopal Church, which still imposes itself grandly on Queen's Gardens – and the discovery must have taken place some time before the second opening of the vault, which is clearly dated to September 1868. Many years later, the Episcopal clergyman related the events around the first discovery in a letter to Thomas Truman Oliphant – one of the most prominent of St Andrews' citizens at the time. Oliphant showed the letter to Linskill, who reproduced it within a letter of his own written to the *Aberdeen Weekly Journal* (and other papers) on 9 February 1894. This is what Skinner wrote:

> I remember looking at some stonemasons repairing the Abbey wall, near the lighthouse tower… A chisel belonging to one of the workmen fell through an interstice and disappeared. I urged the men to take out some of the stones of the wall, when, lo! We found a vault in the interior, and, striking a light, we discovered a coffin with a roof-shaped lid, which had partly fallen off, and inside was the form of a female dressed in satin, which when touched became dust, and on her skeleton hands and forearms she wore long white

kid gauntlet gloves, with numerous buttons. The wall was built up again.

This is what we might call the *ur*-document of the White Lady case: the first eye-witness account of the female corpse, complete with the description of her coffin, rich clothes, and long gloves, all of which played an important role in the subsequent mythologizing of the case. Jesse Hall, the manager of the town gas works and the local inspector for the Woods and Forest Department (the official body charged with clearing up the cathedral ruins), thought that the mason present was named John Ainslie.

Word got around, and soon Mr Hall found himself approached by pair of antiquaries keen to investigate further: Mr Smith, a watchmaker, and Mr Walker, the University Librarian. Despite his distaste for disturbing the dead, the inspector eventually agreed to a brief and discreet investigation. So, before six in the morning of 7 September 1868, the three men (accompanied by a mason and his teenaged apprentice) opened up part of the doorway into the upper chamber of the tower. These are Smith's notes from the event, as reproduced by Linskill in the *Haunted Tower* pamphlet:

> We found it a square chamber with a recess westward in the body of the wall, in which was a number of coffins containing bodies, the coffins being piled one over the other. The bodies – about ten in number – which we examined were in a wonderful state of preservation. They had become dried and sufficiently stiff to be lifted up and set on end.

This suggests that Smith and Walker *et al* propped the preserved bodies up against the walls themselves (later writers have

The Haunted Tower in relation to the east gable of the ruined cathedral. (Photo by Geoff Holder)

claimed that the cadavers were already upright when the explorers arrived, but this is clearly not the case).

The watchmaker's description continued:

> One of them, a female, had on her hands white leather gloves, very entire, a piece of which Carmichael took away as a relic.

Smith remembered the name of the mason as being Mr T. Carmichael, whereas Jesse Hall was convinced it was the same John Ainslie who had been present at the original discovery. Hall's memory may be more accurate, as some years later the mason's apprentice, John Grieve, made the following statement:

> I assisted John Ainslie to open the tower. I then saw the body of a woman, with a silk napkin tied round her head. She was lying on the floor of the chamber, and the coffin was sticking about three feet above,

and the bottom had fallen out. She was in a state of perfect preservation, and had long black hair; otherwise she was quite devoid of clothing. I saw no gloves.

Mr Walker, for his part, appears to have left no record of his recall of the events, but Jesse Hall did remember what occurred that early morning:

> We all scrambled in, and by the light of a candle, which we carried, we saw two chests lying side by side. I cannot say how many chests there were. We did not want to disturb them any more than we could help. There would be half-a-dozen as far as I can remember. I saw the body of a girl. The body was stiff and mummified-like. What appeared to be a glove was on one of the hands.

John Grieve may not have seen the gloves that the Revd Skinner, Mr Hall and Mr

Smith all mentioned, but it is clear someone did help himself to a souvenir, as, decades later, the surviving fragment of one of the gloves was shown to Linskill, who tells us no more about what subsequently happened to it. Linskill was unclear whether the glove was taken during the first or the second opening of the chamber, and this does point to the souvenir-hunter being John Ainslie. Note that the witnesses disagreed about the number of bodies and coffins present. This may of course be a result of the hurried, cramped viewing conditions where the only light was provided by a candle, but discrepancies such as this can easily arise when the memory is recounted many years later, and so we should be wary of taking all of these reminiscences at face value.

However, it is clear from the accounts we have from three witnesses to the opening on 7 September 1868, that the upper chamber of the Haunted Tower contained at least six – if not ten – bodies. The corpses were well preserved, and one female specimen still had its long hair, as well as some form of textile remains in the form of gloves. There were a number of coffins present, and at least some appeared to have partly disintegrated. Mr Smith further asserted that some of the coffins were made of oak, and a number had a top ridge that indicated a great age.

One of the truly strange things about the 1868 event is that while Messrs Hall, Grieve and Smith are quite clear that only they, plus masons Walker and Ainslie, were present, many years later Matthew Forster Heddle, a Professor of Chemistry at the University, gave his own eye-witness account. He told Linskill and others that he looked through the hole into the upper chamber, and saw the piled-up coffins and one of the bodies, the head of which appeared to have broken off. He also said that he had studied a large number of skulls recovered from the *lower* chamber of the Haunted Tower. This is the first time that we have a mention of anything beyond the bodies found in the *upper* chamber. Of these skulls, the teeth were in excellent condition, and about a dozen had their lower jaws tied up with silk bandana handkerchiefs. All of which is intriguing, and we want to know more, but these skulls appear to have vanished – although perhaps they are lying, ignored and mislabelled, in a dusty draw somewhere. Heddle died in 1897. Many years later, his words were reported in the *Haunted Tower* pamphlet. He, like Walker, was a member of the St Andrews Literary and Philosophical Society, so perhaps he had heard about the expedition via the grapevine and just decided to pop in.

We are not told how long the party remained in the chamber, but if they wanted to avoid public interest, it could not have been long, so presumably by seven a.m. or so, the masons were once more sealing up the gap in the wall (the hole had been made deliberately small, just wide enough for a man to squeeze through). All present agreed not to divulge what they had seen. 'We kept the matter a profound secret,' said Mr Hall, 'and I did not know that anyone knew of it except ourselves.'

The Midnight Re-opening of the Tower

That was the state of affairs in 1868. But at least one of the men present that morning clearly was not altogether discreet, for after a while rumours began to circulate. Linskill, writing in the *Aberdeen Weekly Journal* on 9 February 1894, described how he first heard a garbled account as a boy – a tutor told him that, 'there were a lot of girls found in the turret, in riding dresses and gloves, with no appearance of decay about them'. In later years, an older man told him that the incorruptible body of a beautiful female saint lay in the tower, while a Presbyterian minister and a gamekeeper each separately informed Linskill that they had seen the 'mummies'. It appeared that neither the Haunted Tower nor its secret contents were secure. Then in 1888, Linskill got hold of John Grieve – now a master mason – learned his story, and vowed to launch his own investigation. Finally, after pulling enough strings, the Dean of Guild gained the necessary permissions, and engaged Mr Grieve to once again dismantle part of the entrance into the upper tower. The Dean briefly alluded to 'other friends' being present, but he did not name them in print. It was 21 August 1888, almost twenty years to the day since the 1868 expedition. Linskill, with his customary flair for the dramatic, decided to stage the entry at midnight.

The adventurers, however, were to be disappointed. Inside, all was chaos and destruction. The coffins were in tiny fragments. A few skulls and skeletons remained, but there was no sight of any of the 'mummies'. Hay and straw were scattered around, as if someone had been packing items into boxes – the preserved young woman was nowhere to be found. Clearly, sometime between 1868 and 1888, someone else had broken in and desecrated the remains of the dead.

The Aftermath – 1894 and All That

Who could have been the culprits? The finger was pointed at the student body, although with little more than rumour and conjecture to support the accusation. Then on 31 January 1894 a letter in the Edinburgh *Evening Dispatch* claimed to throw light on the mystery. It purported to be the gist of a conversation between a St Andrews captain and the author, who signed himself 'Interested Reader'. The skipper said that, one night, he and some medical students had broken into a sealed tower and stolen, 'A female body which was in a state of complete preservation. The body was that of a good-looking girl with black hair.' The preserved corpse had been locked up in a cellar, but the captain then succumbed to a handsome bribe to deliver the body to a rival antiquarian. At this point the skipper heard no more of the female cadaver. It is impossible to say whether this story is authentic or whether it was an imaginative product of the recent furore.

And a furore there was. In January 1894, *The Saturday Review* had published an article entitled 'The True Story of the Cathedral Turret'. Principally concerned with the recent pseudo-archaeological investigations into subterranean passages at St Andrews, at its conclusion it added a truly sensational epilogue about the original opening of the Haunted Tower by the antiquarians:

> One of the party squeezed in his head and shoulders, and all of him, in fine, but his feet. Suddenly these became quite rigid; and his friends, pulling him out, found that he had fainted. While he was being attended to, a second man peered into the black hole, in like manner; and he, too, was pulled out in a very ill way. Finally a professor of the United College forced his entire person into the cavity, and did not faint; but presently reappeared with the corpse of a woman in his arms, from which the life seemed to have gone but that hour.

Fainting antiquarians! Black holes! Heroic academics! Preserved dead women! Crikey. Shame it was all a load of hooey. The writer had clearly heard about the 1868 expedition, and decided to 'improve' the details so much that it ended up more like *Indiana Jones and the Secret Chamber of Mummified Babes*. But the *Saturday Review* was not yet finished with its fictionalised tale:

> The turret was now fully explored; and, sitting round in a circle, were found twelve bodies, decked as a feast, and all of them untouched by decay. The professor on the instant sent off to the Lord-Advocate asking what course he should take. The answer came to close it up immediately if he should avoid prosecution. And this was done and the matter hushed up.

The article fallaciously concluded with a note that, when the chamber had been opened again in recent years, all the preserved corpses were still in place: 'At a certain point from St Regulus Tower, all the dead that sleep beneath its shadow are lying as they lay on their death-bed.'

As was customary at the time, the article from the *Saturday Review* was circulated, verbatim, in numerous newspapers, creating a great deal of interest. On 1 February 1894, Linskill wrote to the *Aberdeen Weekly Journal* and other papers, thoroughly refuting the report, and providing many of the details about the 1868 investigation given above. A week later, the Dean of Guild was back in print, giving further chapter and verse on how the *Saturday Review* claims were all nonsense. But the damage had been done. The periodical was popular and influential, and January and February 1894 saw the tale of the Haunted Tower move out of the exclusive purlieu of a few St Andrews antiquarians, and into the letters columns of the *Scotsman* and many other newspapers. The nation now knew about the Haunted Tower, and the cosy world of St Andrews ghost lore would never be the same again.

Enter the White Lady

There is no verifiable link between the White Lady and the lady of the Haunted Tower. They may be connected, but they could equally be brought together by coincidence and the human hunger for a satisfying narrative. Tellingly, Linskill revealed in the *Haunted Tower* pamphlet that when he first came to St Andrews in the 1870s, he picked up many stories about the White Lady, but did not connect her with the Tower Lady, so clearly his informants were not yet making that link. A resident of Abbey Walk told the avid ghost-hunter that she often saw a female phantom dressed in white moving across the top of the Abbey wall – the location where the parapet walk once ran. This, I very much suspect, is the same elderly informant who appeared in *St Andrews Ghost Stories*, in which she related an episode from her childhood in the 1820s or '30s:

> A lot of us had been out at Kinkell Braes one afternoon and stayed there long past the time allowed us. It was almost dark, and we scuttled up the brae from the Harbour rather frightened. Just near the turret light we saw the lady gliding along the top of the old Abbey wall. She was robed in a grey white dress with a veil over her head. She had raven black hair, and a string of beads hanging from her waist. We all huddled together, with our eyes and mouths wide open, and watched the figure… She went inside the parapet wall at the Haunted Tower and vanished completely.

The woman's sister had also seen the spectre on one of the turrets in the Abbey wall. The *Haunted Tower* pamphlet also mentions three fisherman walking up from the harbour one moonlit night when, through the iron gate in the Abbey wall, they saw a woman in white walking along the path. Their initial idea – that she must have been accidentally locked in the grounds – was soon dispelled when she passed right through the bars of the locked gate. The fishermen told Linskill that one of them had fainted on the spot, while the other two dropped their creels and fled. If all these reminiscences are accurate, they point to multiple witnesses seeing the phantom, long before the secrets of the Haunted Tower were suspected.

It is not clear when the legend of the White Lady became intertwined with the narrative of the preserved woman in the Haunted Tower. I suspect that when the preserved bodies in the Haunted Tower became an open secret, the existing ghost story gained an additional dimension – a real female corpse to tie the tale to, and a mummy at that. It was a supernatural storytelling match made in heaven.

I can, however, find no further recorded sightings of the White Lady in the later nineteenth century – unless, of course, she is the same spectre as the Veiled Nun of St Leonard's, for whom see Chapter 2. *St Andrews Ghost Stories,* which came out in 1911, has numerous references to the White Lady, and these episodes perfectly illustrate the frustrations that characterise Linskill's work. On the one hand, we have the old woman's childhood reminiscence, as quoted above. And on the other, Linskill gives us a *faux* M.R. James-style fantasy, in which an intrepid chap named Ashton is taken through a subterranean labyrinth beneath the cathedral ruins, his loquacious guide being Thomas Plater, the ghostly wicked monk (see Chapter 3). At one point the duo pass a woman dressed as a bride for a wedding. 'Fear not,' says the monk, 'that is the White Lady, she can materialise herself and appear when she chooses, but she is not re-incarnate as I am.' Ashton slips and falls unconscious, only to be saved by the White Lady. 'She had a lovely face, but as pale as white marble. She laid an icy cold hand on my hot brow, and then all was darkness again.' With its heavy-handed style and its obvious debt to Linskill's obsession with secret underground passages, this is one of the book's more obvious leaps into fantasy.

Possibly, somewhere between the two extremes of make-believe and memory, is another undated episode from *St Andrews Ghost Stories.* Linskill says the manager of a large theatrical company told him the tale, as they shared the waiting room at King's Cross Station. Some ten years previously, the man was taking an evening stroll on Kirkhill, past the Abbey wall, after dinner when he saw a woman in a long, flowing white dress, with dark hair hanging down past her waist. She vanished near the Haunted Tower. Some time later the witness was passing the same spot with his sister when, in the faint moonlight, they both saw the White Lady:

> We saw the soft trailing dress and the long, black wavy hair. There was something like a rosary hanging from her waist, and a cross or a locket hanging round her throat. As she passed she turned her head towards us, and we both noticed her beautiful features, especially her brilliant eyes. She vanished, as before, near that old tower.

One of the factors that seem to distinguish Linskill's fantasies from actual tales he was told by real people, is the way he uses personal names. Episodes that are obviously ludicrous tend have named narrators, although, of course, the names are made up. The adventure that 'Ashton' had with the Wicked Monk and the White Lady, mentioned above, is an obvious example. In contrast, a number of less elaborate ghostly experiences are usually entirely anonymous, as if Linskill did not want to identify a specific individual (the elderly lady who saw the White Lady in her childhood is characterised in this way). The narrator of the tale told at King's Cross is not named, and so, in this case, Linskill may have actually been reporting an experience that had really originated from another person's memory. Peter Underwood's *Gazetteer of Scottish Ghosts* briefly mentions that, when she was fourteen years of age, a Mrs Stevenson of Elgin, together with her brother, had seen the ghost in the Abbey on a moonlit night. I wonder if Mrs Stevenson was the sister of Linskill's theatrical manager friend, or whether she and her brother were from a much later period altogether.

If we can assume that Linskill's later informants were discussing events from the last two decades of the Victorian era, and the first ten years of the twentieth century, then, at least as far as I can tell, the White Lady was not reported again for more than another fifty years. On 25 May 1968, the *St Andrews Citizen* ran a story that began, 'The White Lady walks again.' Alison Grant, an arts student from Rotterdam, and Mark Hedges, a medical student from Bedford, told the reporter that the previous week they had seen the motionless figure of the White Lady beside one of the round towers in the precinct wall. 'She was wearing a long bright white dress with a simple veil,' said Miss Grant. 'Her features were not distinguishable at all. She seemed to have quite

long hands. Her arms were clasped in front of her body below waist level and she was holding a book.' Mr Hedges added that he thought the stationary woman looked as if she was carved out of sandstone. Alison Grant had seen the ghost three times before, the first occasion being in November 1966, long before she had heard the legend of the White Lady.

In June 1979, ghost-hunter Andrew Green travelled to St Andrews to interview Ian MacDonald and his wife. Some four years earlier, the couple had been looking round the cathedral ruins when they both saw a woman in a light grey dress, carrying what looked like a prayer book, and with her face obscured by a light veil. 'You don't see that these days,' said Mr MacDonald. At which point the figure vanished near the Haunted Tower. The episode was recorded in Green's book *Ghosts of Today*.

Summarising these accounts, the White Lady is described as: veiled, or unveiled; carrying a book, or not; possessing a rosary or a string of beads, or not; having long black hair, or not; walking, or motionless; passing through solid objects, or vanishing; moving through the grounds of the cathedral, or outside the precinct wall, or along the top of the wall itself; and seen by moonlight, or at twilight, or in the evening, or in daylight. The only consistent features are that the phantom is female, clothed in a long white or grey-white dress, and silent. There would appear to be no further recorded sightings of the White Lady since 1975, despite the fact that, thanks to popular journalism and the internet, she now has celebrity status.

Attempts to identify the White Lady

It is a truth universally acknowledged that a single ghost in possession of a good reputation must be in want of a name. Several attempts have been made to identify the preserved young woman in the Haunted Tower, and, by extension, the White Lady. The suggestions tend to reveal the romantic tendencies of those involved, rather than an adherence to mundane historical fact. On 8 February 1894, an antiquarian, Mr A. Hutcheson, wrote a long and involved letter to the *St Andrews Citizen,* in which he suggested that the lady of the tower was either the Pictish Princess Muren, who in untrustworthy legend was supposedly the first Christian to be buried at St Andrews, or a local saint, whose embalmed body was hidden here to protect it from the Reformation mob in 1559. Linskill's informants twice suggested the spirit was one of the 'Queen's Maries' or the 'Four Marys', the noblewomen who attended Mary, Queen of Scots, although Linskill himself never made it clear whether this was supposed to be Mary Livingstone, Mary Fleming, Mary Beaton or Mary Seaton – none of whom perished or were buried in St Andrews. The historical net has been flung even wider, taking in everyone from a discarded mistress of Cardinal Beaton (*see* Chapter 3) to the Cardinal's *de facto* wife, Marion Ogilvie.

There is not a single element in any of the sightings that could align the White Lady with any of the suggestions put forward above. Attention has focused on princesses, saints and noblewomen because these are all figures of romance; but the White Lady, should she be real, is just as likely to be a person unknown to history.

The Lady of the Plague

When the explorers of 1868 inspected the coffins, they found no identifying plaques,

and this lack of identification helped fuel the speculation cited above. However, in 1912, David Henry published *Sketches of Medieval St Andrews*, in which he deciphered a badly defaced mural carving on the tower. The heraldry indicated the Clephane family, while the letters 'K' and 'C' could be made out. The monument was erected to the memory of Katharine Clephane, wife of John Martine, Laird of Denbrae. The date was 1609.

Denbrae is in the parish of Logie, between Cupar and Kilmany, west of Balmullo and Leuchars. Walter Macfarlane's *Genealogical Collections Concerning Families in Scotland*, written in 1750, tells us that in 1567 John Martine married 'Catharine Clepane Daughter to [unknown] Clepane of Carslogie and sister to Mr George Clepane and Margaret spouse to John Anstruther of that Ilk'. Both Laird Martine and Mistress Clephane were well-connected amongst the Fife gentry.

It is not clear when Katherine Clephane died; the monument on the tower has the date 1609, but her husband John Martine (now not just a laird, but a Baillie of St Andrews) married Sibilla Wardlaw before his own death in 1608 – Katherine must have passed away before that date. Katherine Clephane would have been in her sixties at the time of her death. She is an unlikely candidate for the preserved corpse whose beauty struck those who entered the sealed chamber.

But there are other possibilities. Katherine Clephane and John Martine had one son, George, and three daughters – Margaret, Christian and a third whose name was illegible in Macfarlane's original manuscript. Margaret went on to marry a man named David Carstairs, but Christian and her unknown sister both died in the plague that struck St Andrews in July 1605.

The word 'plague' did not necessarily always entail the Black Death, or bubonic plague. At the time, it could refer to bacillary dysentery or other serious epidemics. Outbreaks of 'plague' hit St Andrews in 1350, 1362, 1529, 1568, 1585, 1605, 1647, 1665 and 1667. The plague pits, where the bodies were buried in mass graves, used to be on The Scores, just west of the present St James' Church. Bones were dug up here in 1906, 1909 and 1987.

Can we assume that the wealthy Martine family somehow managed to avoid having their daughters consigned to the mass graves? Of course, this cannot be proved, because the law did state that victims of plague had to be disposed of in the regulated manner, in an attempt to limit the contagion. It is possible that a number of the Martine/Clephane family grouping, including Katharine, succumbed to the epidemic, and their corpses were walled up in the tower at the same time. On the other hand, perhaps the vault had been in use as a family mausoleum for a number of years, and it was the coming of the plague that saw its final use and closure. Or, possibly, none of those whose skeletons were later discovered, ever died from the plague and the family vault simply went out of use. We have no idea when the chamber was sealed for the final time. I suspect that the carved monument to Katherine Clephane was erected by her son, George, who after 1620 went on to become Provost of St Salvator's College. One of the coffined bodies almost certainly was that of Katherine Clephane; perhaps the female corpse with the long raven-black hair, a dress of fine material, and white arm-length leather gloves, may indeed have belonged to Christian Martine or her unnamed sister. We will never know.

Relics and Remains

Also unknown is the reason why the bodies in the tower came to exist in a state of preservation. During the kerfuffle of 1894, several commentators suggested that the bodies had been deliberately embalmed; much more likely was that the environmental conditions within the chamber somehow arrested the normal processes of decay – something similar can be found in the preserved medieval bodies in the crypt of St Michan's Church in Dublin. Of course, with the St Andrews bodies spirited away, we have no evidence either way. Their state of preservation was not entire

The entrance to the lower chamber, where the skulls were found. (Photo by Geoff Holder)

– the Revd Skinner spoke of the arms and forearms beneath the leather gloves as being 'skeletonised' – but skin and hair does appear to have been preserved on more than one body.

When William Linskell left the desecrated chamber in August 1888, a small number of skulls, skeletons and coffin shards remained, pushed out of sight in the corner. These have all long vanished, and no-one knows to where. At some point over the next few years, the walling at the entrance to the upper chamber was replaced with an iron grille, which is still in place. None of the other body parts, clothing or other items from the Haunted Tower have come to light.

With one possible exception. From at least 1894 a preserved foot was on display in the museum run by the Literary and Philosophical Society. In 1896, in one of his regular columns for *Longman's Magazine,* Andrew Lang described the relic:

> In the College Museum is a beautiful foot of a woman, an exquisite thing…

It is reported to have come out of the Haunted Tower, but nobody seems really to know the truth.

It was a mystery indeed, as there was another candidate for the foot: an Egyptian mummy. In 1807, James Grierson, writing in his book *Delineations of St. Andrews*, toured the King James Library on South Street:

> Among the curiosities shewn to strangers who visit this library, is an Egyptian mummy but in a bad state of preservation.

Quite incredibly, the preserved foot mentioned in 1894 is still in existence. It is in the University's Anatomy and Pathology collection and is regularly used in teaching sessions on the structure of the foot. Is it part of the Egyptian mummy, which disintegrated so badly in the nineteenth century that now only a bandaged head remains? Or is it the only physical remnant of the Lady of the Tower, and hence a link, however tenuous, with the White Lady?

2

A Haunted Cluster

The Ghosts of the Pends, St Leonard's School and Queen Mary's House

The neighbourhood of the Pends is a
haunted region.

Russell Kirk, *St Andrews*, 1954

who lived there for several months in 1562.
A bedroom on the top floor is said to have
been the Queen's.

HE area immediately south-west of
the Cathedral may have the claim
to being the part of St Andrews
with the greatest concentration of ghost
stories. Within this compact historic rec-
tangle, there is an extraordinary cluster
of reported hauntings spread over several
separate buildings, and stretching across five
centuries to the present day. At the very end
of South Street is The Pends (more strictly
The Pends Gatehouse), the original vaulted
entrance into the monastic precinct, now
roofless but still awe-inspiring. From here
Pends Road runs down to the Harbour,
passing between the Eastern Cemetery and
high walls, but just a short distance from the
gatehouse, a lane, known as the Nun's Walk,
runs west to the grounds of St Leonard's
public school and the medieval St Leonard's
Chapel. The L-shaped public right of way
past the chapel brings you back to South
Street – and just to the east is a sixteenth-
century building widely known as 'Queen
Mary's House' after Mary, Queen of Scots,

The Ghosts of the Pends

In the nineteenth century the track
through the medieval gatehouse became
a public road, which necessitated the rais-
ing of the roadway level by more than two
feet, and the removal of the cross-wall
and the jambs of the vaulting, because
of the hazard to vehicles. Nevertheless,
its fifteenth-century structure, seventy-
eight feet long with walls four-and-a-half
feet thick, still bleeds a powerful sense of
atmosphere. If you are taking photographs,
watch out for the traffic.

We have an unusual report from The
Pends, dating from the early 1950s. Russell
Kirk was a visiting US academic who later
went on to become the 'grandfather' of
American Conservatism – his political
works were a great influence on Ronald
Reagan, for example. In his 1954 book
St Andrews, he described how one moon-
less autumn midnight he was walking up
the darkened Pends Road from the harbour

A Victorian view of the Pends Gatehouse. Note how the artist has diminished the height of the people to exaggerate the scale of the arch. (From MacGibbon and Ross, The ecclesiastical architecture of Scotland, *1896)*

The interior of the gatehouse today. (Photo by Geoff Holder)

The Pends Road. To the right of the photograph is the gatehouse, and the Nun's Walk is on the left. (Photo by Geoff Holder)

The jetty – site of Fay Weldon's encounter with 'the preacher'. (Photo by Geoff Holder)

when he became aware of someone keeping pace with him from the opposite side of the road. The figure was 'so shadowy as to be more movement than definite form', and he could not make out the face, the gender or even the shape of the enigmatic pedestrian, who followed him into the even darker gatehouse. Gratefully moving away from the unknown of the darkness into the bright streetlamps of South Street, Kirk waited for his companion to emerge from the gatehouse. No-one appeared, and there was no alternative exit. At this point, Kirk realised that although his own feet had been clearly moving through noisy gravel, his fellow-traveller's paces had been silent throughout. It may be, of course, that, despite the lack of moonlight or streetlamps in The Pends, Kirk had somehow cast an amorphous shadow, and mistaken it for another being; but the academic was convinced he had had a brush with the supernatural.

Perhaps this phantom of The Pends was the same apparition seen by novelist Fay Weldon, as described in an article she wrote for the *Daily Mail* on 18 August 2000. One quiet evening, during her student days, Weldon visited the harbour, which is reached via the Pends Road. She walked out onto the far end of the jetty and then turned to go back. For some reason, she looked behind her to the jetty terminus. Of course, no-one should have been there – as she had been alone there a few seconds ago – and there was no other access. But standing at the jetty end was a man in a black cloak and a broad-brimmed black hat. The mysterious figure started to follow the young student. She quickened her pace, and he matched it. She started to run. So did the mysterious man. But when Weldon looked back once more, the figure had vanished. Local enquiries revealed this apparition to be known by the name of 'the preacher'. The harbour area was his preserve. Sometimes he appeared as a full figure. But on other occasions, all that could be seen is his shadow – marked by his distinctive broad-brimmed hat.

Yet another phantom clergyman is recorded in Helen Cook's 1983 book *A Haunting of Ghosts*. Cook knew St Andrews well, and, I suspect, garnered some of her ghost stories from her father – a policeman in the town. Unfortunately this episode is not given a specific location or date, and there are no other verifiable details. Many years earlier, on a stormy August night, a young man was walking home around 2 a.m. when he saw someone standing on a path behind a closed gate. To the witness' horror, the figure passed straight through the iron bars of the gate, without opening it, then – with a slow and deliberate pace – walked towards him. Moonlight briefly shone out from behind the clouds, revealing the figure to be dressed in the clerical garb of a vanished age, but his clothes – completely dry, despite the recent downpours – gave off a vile, musty smell, and the apparition projected a distinct air

of evil. The witness was overcome by fear and only 'came to' when he was woken up by a policeman who had seen him standing in the street, staring into space as if in a trance or altered state.

James Wilkie's 1931 book *Bygone Fife from Culross to St Andrews* has another episode from The Pends, although the details are scant. In the 1920s, an unnamed female visitor to St Andrews was walking through the gatehouse when she passed a woman clad in fifteenth-century dress with her face concealed. The visitor assumed this was a participant in a pageant or costume ball, and, being something of an expert on historic costume, admired the details of the lady's antique clothing. Upon enquiry, the visitor was assured that no fancy-dress event was being held in St Andrews – and she was also told, in no uncertain terms, that she had been lucky indeed that the figure had remained covered, for if the veil

The Nun's Walk and the entrance to St Leonard's School. (Photo by Geoff Holder)

had been lifted, then she might have suffered a terrible fate.

Wilkie called the apparition 'The Lady of The Pends', although she normally attracts the sobriquet of 'The Veiled Nun'. She's famous, is the Veiled Nun, although her fame – as disseminated through websites, tour-guide tales and popular accounts – originates, once again, in the pages of *St Andrews Ghost Stories*. Linskill tells us that, in the mid-sixteenth century, a beautiful woman who lived in South Street was so fed up with fending off would-be husbands that she resolved to become a nun. On hearing this, her most ardent suitor resolved, with her parents' approval, to marry her straight away. But when he arrived in St Andrews, he found that the woman preferred mutilation to marriage:

> Sooner than be an earthly bride, she had mutilated her face by slitting her nostrils; she had cut off her eyelids and both her top and bottom lips, and had branded her fair cheeks with cruel hot irons.

The rejected youth committed suicide and the heartbroken woman took the veil. Her spirit, according to Linskill, still walked the lane from The Pends to St Leonard's:

> She is all dressed in black, with a long black veil over the once lovely face, and carries a lantern in her hand. Should any bold visitor to that avenue meet her, she slowly sweeps her face veil aside, raises the lantern to her scarred face, and discloses those awful features to his horrified gaze.

Linskill gave an example of the effect such a revelation could have on a witness. A recent Cambridge graduate he called Talbot supposedly encountered the Nun one night in the lane, promptly fainting in horror.

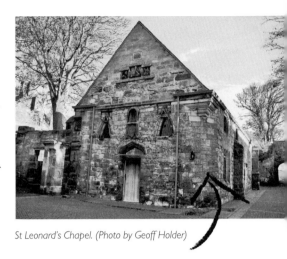
St Leonard's Chapel. (Photo by Geoff Holder)

The vision haunted him for the rest of his days, and he died of heart failure a mere two years later.

There is something of a problem with this tale, and it's not just Linskill's usual unreliability. The story of the beautiful young woman who mutilates her face to avoid either marriage or sexual assault – what might be termed a 'heroine of virginity' – is millennia-old, being known in Classical times. In the Christian tradition, St Eusebia, and forty of her nuns at the monastery of St Cyr in Marseilles, all cut off their noses to prevent being raped by the Saracen invaders, who, upon seeing them, promptly massacred the entire group. This took place in the year 738 AD. Similarly, around 870 AD, St Ebba and the nuns of Coldingham monastery in Berwickshire, sliced off their noses and upper lips when the Vikings attacked, while similar events occurred in the tenth century at the abbey of St Florentine in Spain, and the convent of St Clare in Acri, Italy in 1291 AD. In all cases, the self-mutilants escaped rape but were massacred wholesale, thus becoming martyrs of the church.

Saintly would-be nuns who employed self-inflicted rhinotomy to avoid marriage, included the twelfth-century St Oda of Hainault, and St Margaret of Hungary, a century later. In the late sixteenth century, in Peru, St Rose of Lima followed a similar course of action so that she could be a nun and not a wife. On the more folkloric religious level, numerous female saints supposedly received temporary divine disfigurement so that they could avoid marriage and become nuns; once the woman was a Bride of Christ, the deformity or impairment vanished. These stories are told of St Brigid in Ireland, and numerous French saints, including St Fara, St Enymia, St Angadresima, St Gisla, and St Ulphia (more examples can be found in *Forgetful of their sex: female sanctity and society, ca. 500-1100*, by Jane Tibbetts Schulenburg). In other words, the 'marriage-avoiding self-mutilating nun' is a well-known theme with both historical and folkloric credentials, and is sufficiently gruesome for anyone wanting to invent a dramatic ghostly tradition.

In the St Leonard's case, the legend of the Veiled Nun has no checkable details. And there was no nunnery at St Andrews. Well, not quite. At some point in the late fifteenth or early sixteenth century, the number of pilgrims coming to St Andrews dropped off drastically. The Priory Guest House thus underwent a change of use, becoming a hospice or sanctuary for poor old women. These do not appear to have been nuns as such, as there is no record of any kind of convent administration. The Guest House stood on a site now occupied by St Leonard's School. In 1912, the local antiquarian, David Henry, suggested that some of the architectural features in the nearby St Leonard's Church indicated there was a time when only women worshipped in the chapel. St Leonard's had been a parish church since at least 1413, open to all. But there was a blind passage leading from the sacristy into the thickness of the wall. It was suggested that, to keep the priest and the women apart, the holy man read services and heard confessions through a slit or grating linking the blind passage to the main body of the church.

According to the St Andrews historian Hay Fleming, the old women were required, in return for the charity they received, to live a holy life. But apparently 'they showed no great regard either for morality or piety' and so were turfed out, and in 1512 all the buildings on the site became part of the new St Leonard's College. The community of poor old women does not sound like a destination for the fine, beautiful (and wealthy) woman of the Veiled Nun legend, and anyway, the community was disbanded by 1512, while the Veiled Nun supposedly dates from the 1560s. I suggest that this is what really happened: the existing theme of the self-mutilating nun was imported from elsewhere and tacked on to the folk memory of the community of old women who once lived at St Leonard's. It is my contention that the Veiled Nun is little more than a folk ghost, a folkloric creation given further impetus by Linskill's powerfully Gothic narrative. And this creation has been mightily successful. For all the writers of the nineteenth century, the lane leading from The Pends to St Leonard's had no name; but by the time James Wilkie was gathering ghost stories and folklore in 1931, it had become known as the Nun's Walk, a street named for a ghost probably invented out of imagination and wish-fulfilment.

Ah, but if it was only that simple to dismiss the Veiled Nun. Firstly, there is the (admittedly unsatisfactory) account recorded by James Wilkie, as in the previous paragraph. Then there is another report from Wilkie. In around 1929, a female doctor was waiting in the Nun's Walk for a friend who had business to attend to in the school. It was a winter afternoon, with good light. Her two small dogs were scampering about happily – until they both suddenly stopped, fixated on the rusty locked gates that closed off the school end of the lane. Their eyes followed something invisible to human eyes as it advanced down the lane, and as it passed their owner they huddled behind her legs, whining. The dogs continued to follow with their eyes the 'something' as it proceeded towards Pends Road, and, once whatever it was had passed, happily returned to their gambols. It's from the same (possibly credulous) author, and the details are just as vague, but it is worth noting.

And then, just to confuse things, we have a report from the journal *Folklore* in 1944. Local folklorist H.J. Rose noted that the older inhabitants of the area still believed in the ghost, which he described as a nun-like figure who walked The Pends and was known by the name the Grey Lady. In the summer of 1944, a fishing boat had recently capsized, drowning a number of men. For several days the body of the boat's owner was not recovered, and then an old fisherman stated that it would be found the next day because he had seen the Grey Lady standing at the harbour end of Pends Road. Illuminated by moonlight, she was facing the sea with her hands cupped around her mouth, as if calling out to someone, or something. The fisherman interpreted this as her calling for the corpse of the drowned man to return, and, the very next day, the body was indeed recovered.

Here the Grey Lady is not veiled, and is acting in a benevolent, rather than a malevolent, manner. This episode seems to somehow link the Veiled Nun with the White Lady of the Haunted Tower. Are both they and the Grey Lady all expressions of the same phenomenon? Are the White Lady, the Veiled Nun and the Grey Lady simply labels of convenience, three names for the same thing? Or are there two (or more) female ghosts a-wandering in this compact area?

St Leonard's School

St Leonard's public school occupies a vast tract of land bounded by Abbey Street, Abbey Walk, The Shore, Pends Road and South Street. At its core is a roughly L-shaped collection of historic buildings stretching from the eastern end of South Street, south-eastward to Pends Road.

The site has a complex history. For most of the Middle Ages, it hosted a number of ancillary structures belonging to the Priory, such as a guest house for pilgrims, and a granary. These were enclosed within the great mile-long Precinct Wall, part of which still forms the school's boundary. In the year 1512, many of the Priory buildings were hived off to form St Leonard's College, one of the core colleges of the University. The first students were Augustinian novices studying arts and theology. In 1772, St Leonard's amalgamated with St Salvator's College to form United College, and the buildings of St Leonard's were sold off as a number of high-status private dwellings – although the University retained ownership of the church on the site, St Leonard's Chapel. Then, in 1882, the entire location was purchased to form St Leonard's School – a highly-regarded public school for girls. Since 1999, it has been a co-educational independent school. All these changes of ownership and function have meant that the structures have been successively

An outlook of the buildings of St Leonard's School. (Photo by Geoff Holder)

remodelled, demolished, rebuilt, relocated and otherwise altered, making it at times difficult to reconstruct the earlier geography of this historic corner of the town.

The New Inn or Novum Hospitium

Sadly the first of our allegedly haunted locations no longer exists. The *Novum Hospitium,* or New Inn, once stood on the western side of Pends Road, on the site of the school hospice, behind the current boundary wall. Just north of the site stands the original entrance arch of the New Inn, now presiding over one of the routes into the school grounds. This gateway, however, is not in its original position, having been relocated on two separate occasions in 1845 and 1894, while the remainder of the build-

ing disappeared very early in the nineteenth century. In 'Haunted St Andrews', an article for *The Scots Magazine* in November 1978, author Helen Cook mentioned an event that took place in her grandfather's time. Late one evening, a police sergeant on the beat clearly saw a woman in a green riding habit, ride down Pends Road and right through a solid wall. The spot where she disappeared had once been the entrance to the New Inn.

Constructed in 1537 – probably the last major building project of the Priory before the Reformation – the New Inn was originally intended as a convalescent home for Princess Magdalen of France, the bride of King James V. Sadly the young woman's health was so poor that she died just six weeks after arriving at Holyrood Palace, and so never saw St Andrews (James V later wed Mary of Guise and they honeymooned

31

The former gate of the Novum Hospitium, or New Inn, which is now part of St Leonard's School. (Photo by Geoff Holder)

at the New Inn). Having been built for royalty, the New Inn continued in the same vein, and later housed such distinguished guests as the Earl of Moray, when he was the post-Reformation Commendator of the Priory, King James VI, and a number of archbishops. It may have also hosted Mary, Queen of Scots and John Knox (although at different times). All in all, it was the highest-status accommodation in post-Reformation St Andrews. And this meant that it also had a better class of haunting.

The Wraith of Archbishop Sharp, 1666

The reputation of James Sharp (1613–1679), at least within popular tradition, is that of a turncoat, even a traitor. A well-connected member of the Presbyterian cabal during the turbulent years of the Scottish involvement in the English Civil War, Sharp initially sided with the Covenanters – Scots who wished to defend egalitarian Presbyterianism against the incursions of elite bishops appointed by the rival Episcopalians. Sharp, however, then changed his spots, and supported King Charles II and his re-ordering of the Scottish church along Episcopal lines – a Protestant church ruled by bishops, these bishops appointed by the King. In return, in 1661, Sharp was appointed Archbishop of St Andrews and Primate of all Scotland – effectively the most powerful religious man in the country. When the Covenanters rebelled against this imposed Episcopalianism, Sharp mercilessly persecuted his former comrades. As such, he became a hate figure, and tales were circulated about his dealings with the Devil. It is within the context of this religious turmoil, and its associated propaganda, that we must assess the following story of the Archbishop's wraith or doppelganger.

In 1666, it was said, Sharp was in Edinburgh, examining the Covenanter prisoners taken at the Pentland Rebellion (many of whom were tortured and suffered horrendous deaths). Requiring some papers to further the case, he dispatched his running footman to St Andrews, with a key to his cabinet. According to the sole description of the events, the servant left Edinburgh at ten in the morning and arrived at his destination at 4 p.m., having covered a distance of some thirty miles on foot in six hours (including the ferry across the Firth of Forth from Leith, to the Fife port of Pettycur). To the footman's surprise, when he opened the Archbishop's door in the New Inn, his employer was already there:

He saw the Bishop sitting at a table near the window, as if he had been reading and writing, with his black gown and tippet, [and] his broad hat, just as he had left him at Edinburgh, which did surprise the fellow at first, though he was not much terrified; …he spake to him merrily thus, 'Ho! my Lord! Well ridden, indeed! I am sure I left you at Edinburgh at ten o'clock, and yet you are here before me! I wonder that I saw you not pass by me!'

The figure of Sharp looked over his shoulder and gave the servant an angry glance, so the footman ran back downstairs to fetch the Archbishop's Secretary or Chamberlain, who had not seen Sharp arrive.

So they came both up stairs; but before they were fully up, they both saw the Bishop standing upon the stair-head, staring upon them with an angry look, which affrighted them in earnest.

James Sharp, Archbishop of St Andrews 1662-1679. (From Ian Gordon Lindsay, The Cathedrals of Scotland, 1926)

A short while later, the footman returned to the room which was now empty, and, unlocking the cabinet, retrieved the papers. By the following morning he had returned to Edinburgh, where he told Sharp what he had seen; 'Upon which the Bishop, by threats and promises, enjoins him to secrecy.'

On the face of it, this would be a significant sighting, in which two men simultaneously saw the wraith – or *fetch* – of someone they both knew well, while that individual was alive in a distant location. But we must be cautious; the only account of this episode appears in the *Analecta* of the Revd Robert Wodrow, an eighteenth-century Protestant minister sympathetic to the Covenanters (he wrote *The History of the Sufferings of the Church of Scotland from the Restoration to the Revolution,* which is effectively a martyrology for Presbyterians). The *Analecta* – subtitled *Materials for a History of Remarkable Providences, mostly relating to Scotch Ministers and Christians* – displayed Wodrow's keen ear for both ecclesiastical gossip and supernatural tales associated with members of the church. It was written in the 1720s and finally published in 1842. Many later writers found Wodrow unduly credulous.

Wodrow (1679-1734) was writing fifty or sixty years after the event and was told the story by his informant, John Glasford. We do not know where Glasford heard it, or when. Neither the footman nor the Chamberlain are named. There are also some inconsistent details – twice in the episode, we are told the events took place on a day in summer, while the Pentland Rebellion dated from November 1666, and most of the prisoners held in Edinburgh were executed in December of that year. Wodrow also includes two other stories told about Sharp – in one, a so-called seer stated that she had seen the Archbishop communing with Satan, while in the other, Sharp was said to have possessed a demonic familiar in the shape of a humming bee. At no point does Wodrow state that he believes these tales, but there is a distinct whiff of anti-Episcopalian Covenanter propaganda about them. Combined with the lack of checkable details in the original account, I suggest that we treat the story of the Wraith of Archbishop Sharp with advanced scepticism.

James Sharp also contributes one of St Andrews' most enduring ghost stories, a phantom that has been written about for over two centuries. On 3 May 1679, Sharp's brutality towards the Covenanters caught up with him. He was assassinated in his coach as it passed across Magus Moor, some three miles west of St Andrews, on the road from Strathkinness. As a confederate of the Devil, he was believed to be invulnerable to bullets, so the conspirators ran him through with their swords, leaving him with sixteen stab wounds. A monument to Sharp – and to the Covenanters who were randomly selected for execution at the spot in revenge – still stands on Magus Moor.

The setting for Sharp's murder – his magnificent archiepiscopal coach – is what propels the ghost story, both literally and figuratively. The horse-drawn coach is said to be seen and/or heard rattling along the Strathkinness Road, and via South Street and Pends Road – presumably recreating its intended, but never completed, final journey of May 1679, as Sharp would have been returning to the New Inn. The hoary tale has gathered mossy legends over the years: supposedly, it runs noiselessly on the cobblestones; to witness it is to be warned of your own forthcoming death; and it casts no shadow. All these are common, even mandatory, elements of standard 'phantom coach' stories, and their Gothic quality reeks of fireside storytelling and fictional ghost tales. Just to complicate matters, the carriage is sometimes ascribed not to Archbishop Sharp but to another controversial (and murdered) churchman, Cardinal Beaton (whom we will meet

The assassination of Archbishop Sharp by Covenanters on Magus Moor. Note the coach to the right of the illustration. (From Charles Rogers, History of St Andrews, *1849)*

in Chapter 3). Thus we have this rhyme, quoted in James K. Robertson's book *About St Andrews – And About*:

Have you heard how the Cardinal's coach goes by,
At dead of night, when the tide is high?
And the moon has hid, and the wind is shrill,
And all the city lies dark and still?

Do we actually have any reliable sightings of this phantom coach? Linskill, not surprisingly, includes an alleged eye-witness report from one of his friends, 'Carson', in *St Andrews Ghost Stories*, but, given the source, you may have your own opinions on the veracity of that account. Carson, according to Linskill, was in St Andrews for the golfing. One humid and stormy night, he went for a midnight stroll along the road to Strathkinness. There he saw an extraordinary sight:

A coach, dark, heavy, primitive; it seemed to have four large black horses, and the driver was a muffled, shapeless figure. It approached with a low humming or buzzing sound, which was most peculiar and unpleasant to hear. The horses made a hollow kind of ticking sound with their feet, otherwise it was noiseless.

The nocturnal pedestrian also noticed a 'coffin-shaped box on the roof' and 'a ghastly white face' peering through the coach window. Despite the moonlight, the vehicle cast no shadow. As it passed him, Carson was gripped with a paralyzing, death-like fear, and he later learned his brother had died in Australia at approximately the same time. His tale was rounded off in suitable Gothic blood-curdling fashion:

It bodes no one any good, and I pity with all my heart anyone who meets it. Beware of those roads late at night, or, like me, you may some day to your injury meet that ghastly, uncanny, old phantom coach. If so, you will remember it to your dying day.

Another encounter is related in Helen Cook's 1983 book *A Haunting of Ghosts*. At an unspecified date in the twentieth century, an unnamed resident of St Andrews heard a carriage rumbling along South Street at 1.30 a.m. It is possible this had a plausible explanation, but the man connected it to stories he had heard of Sharp's carriage, and mentioned it to friends. The coach was traditionally said to appear on the anniversary of the Archbishop's death, the 3rd of May. The witness had heard the carriage on 14 May – but an adjustment to the British calendar in 1752, 'lost' eleven days, so that Wednesday, 2 September 1752 was followed by Thursday, 14 September 1752. By this calculation, the coach had been heard on the 'real' anniversary of the assassination.

There is, however, an entirely different (but still ghostly) potential source for the sound of a supernatural horse-drawn carriage in South Street – see below, in the section on Queen Mary's House, for an alternative to 'Sharp's Phantom Carriage'.

Archbishop Ross and the Ghosts

After Sharp was murdered in 1679, the post of the Archbishop of St Andrews was taken by Alexander Burnet. On Burnet's death in 1684, it was Arthur Ross (also known as Rose) who became Archbishop and occupied the New Inn. Ross was, in addition, the

Chancellor of the University of St Andrews; he was also the last Archbishop of the See, because a change of government in 1689 abolished Episcopacy. From then on, Scotland was officially a Presbyterian nation, and bishops were consigned to the minority (and often proscribed) Episcopalian fringe.

As with Sharp, we owe the ghost story associated with Ross to the Revd Robert Wodrow, this time to a volume published posthumously in 1829, entitled *Private Letters, Now First Printed from the Original Mss., 1694-1732*. If anything, the Ross account is even less satisfactory than the Sharp episode – but it does have the advantage of possessing a named eye-witness.

On 14 January 1718, Thomas Harlaw wrote from Alloa to an acquaintance, the Revd John Warden, who passed the letter on to Wodrow. The text was a tale told to Harlaw by his brother-in-law Andrew Berrage, who, in the 1680s, was Archbishop Ross' principal servant at the New Inn. At that time, there was a room in the house that was widely known to be haunted: 'neither family nor stranger lay in that room, by reason of an old superstition of apparitions that frequented that room' (note: as with the text from *Analecta*, I have here updated the antique spelling to modern usage). Then, one day, so many visitors were staying at the lodging that Berrage was forced to sleep in the haunted room. Noted for his scepticism towards ghosts, Berrage persuaded a young page to share the room – that way, with two witnesses stating that the room was not haunted, it would lose its uncanny reputation, hence becoming once again a liveable room. On the night in question, Berrage and the page banked a good fire, and fell asleep with their backs to each other.

In the middle of the night, Berrage woke to see the coachman coming towards him, while the page was approached from the opposite end of the room by the postillion (the man or boy who rode on one of the horses in a carriage team, while the coachman sat on the actual carriage). The way the description is written, it is clear that both the coachman and his postillion were recognised by Berrage and the page. Berrage – who did not at first think he was addressing some form of apparition – berated the coachman, calling him a 'drunken rascal' and scolding him for coming up to the room and disturbing his sleep. And then came the moment the penny dropped, as Harlaw wrote:

> My brother-in-law rises on his elbow, and swears he would ding the devil out of the coachman, and thrusts at him with a full stroke, till he sees his arm through the apparition, and his hand on the other side of him.

After this revelation, both figures moved back to the walls and 'disappeared like smoke'. After some fervent praying, Berrage and the page discussed what each had seen, sat up frightened in front of the fire for the rest of the night, and decided to say nothing of what had occurred, for fear of scaring the rest of the servants. The story, however, leaked out, and so to persuade his staff that there was nothing to the story, the Archbishop decided to spend the night alone in the 'haunted chamber'. Harlaw takes up the story:

> About the middle of the night, the Bishop comes down stairs with all speed possible, and thought it convenient to bring no thing with him but his shirt, barefooted, calling for his servants; but what he saw he would reveal it to none.

Here the tale ends, and we are left with nothing definite, and no follow-up. Can we credit it with any degree of truth? From the brief notes accompanying the letter, it seems that Thomas Harlaw mentioned the episode to the Revd John Warden in conversation and Warden, knowing of Wodrow's interest in the supernatural, urged Harlaw to write the events down. In relaying his brother-in-law's words, Harlaw was transmitting a memory that must have been more than thirty years' old (as Ross left the New Inn in 1688 or '89). This is plenty of time for an experience to become exaggerated in the mind, and there is no other mention of this episode in any other document from the period. We are not told the name of the page, nor do we learn what scared the Archbishop so.

There is also the curious element that what Berrage and the page saw were not the spirits of the dead, but the fetches or doppelgangers of the living. They saw the coachman and postillion they knew, men who would have at the time presumably been asleep elsewhere in the complex, perhaps in the stables. This is an intriguing parallel with the Sharp case. We do not know whether the episodes from 1666 and the 1680s took place in the same room, but if they did (and both were genuine), does this point to some repeating experience where the apparitions of the living appear in a particular location? Or is it just a load of nonsense, with both the Sharp and Ross events being little more than servants' tittle-tattle? Unfortunately, in each case we have so little to go on that it is impossible to tell.

On 27 January 1904, the *Fife Herald & Journal* published a piece on local ghosts which stated that the ghosts of the New Inn 'so alarmed the people that it had to be pulled down'. The sentiment was amplified in James Wilkie's book of 1931, *Bygone Fife from Culross to St Andrews*:

> In its last years, it was inhabited by a ghost, which so terrified those who ventured within the gates that there remained no other course than to demolish the ill-starred building stone by stone.

This is journalistic hyperbole of the highest degree, as, by the early 1800s, the decaying fabric was simply in the way; but it does indicate the way the old phantoms had become almost venerated in the popular imagination. It is a great pity that we can no longer walk the corridors of the lodging house of kings and archbishops, and investigate what once went on there, and what ghostly apparitions still lurk there.

Sir David Brewster – 'Unaccountable Noises' and Strange Visions

A few dozen yards north-west of the site of the former New Inn, and some thirteen yards south of the present St Leonard's Chapel, stands a much-altered building that was once part of the medieval St Leonard's College. It had once been occupied by George Buchanan, the Principal of the College, a Reformation intellectual who wrote an influential history of Scotland and was appointed as tutor to James VI – ensuring the young King kept on the Protestant straight-and-narrow. When St Leonard's College vacated the grounds, the site served as an upmarket private dwelling, and, in 1838, it became the home of Sir David Brewster – the Principal of United College until 1859. In 1853, he had the building entirely remodelled, so it now bears little resemblance to its original form.

St Leonard's School, with St Leonard's Chapel on the right. (Photo by Geoff Holder)

Brewster (1781–1868) was one of the prominent scientists of the day, specialising in the physics of optics and light. Amongst his many works was *The Stereoscope: Its History, Theory, and Construction*. This 1856 book is credited with the invention of 'spirit photography' – in as much as Brewster casually suggested the way photographic techniques could be used to produce images of 'ghosts' for amusement. By the 1860s and '70s, 'spirit' or 'trick' photography was all the rage – some items being enjoyed as entertainment, while others were used as a 'hard sell' for the claims of spiritualism – the ghostly images were said to be proof that the dead visited us from the afterlife. Brewster was also interested in the nature of illusions and hallucinations. In 1832, he wrote *Letters on Natural Magic*, an admirably sceptically-minded compendium in which he showed that many so-called super-natural events were functions of the way

the human mind or eye operated, or were created by natural forces; the book also suggested ways that the tricks employed by stage magicians could be used to deceive people into thinking they were in touch with the paranormal. In 1855, Brewster witnessed a demonstration in London by the principal medium of the day – the internationally celebrated Daniel Dunglas Home. Much to Home's disappointment, Brewster refused to endorse the rapping and table-lifting as genuinely supernatural, instead suggesting they had been produced by elaborate trick techniques. All of which makes Sir David Brewster an extremely interesting witness when it comes to his own ghostly experiences.

Our testimony comes from one of Brewster's daughters, Margaret Maria Gordon, who wrote *The Home Life of Sir David Brewster* in 1881. According to Ms. Gordon, her father 'really wished to believe in many wonders to which his constitution of mind utterly refused credence.' This tension between the desire to experience genuine marvels and miracles, and the intellectual realisation that such phenomena usually have a natural cause, makes Brewster a particularly modern figure, his position familiar to many present-day Forteans. He also said that he was 'afraid of ghosts, though he did not believe in them'. He enjoyed telling ghost stories to an audience – once causing a young woman to faint in fright – and spent time at sittings with clairvoyants and psychics. A devout Christian, he gave as his opinion that the voices and forms that appeared at séances, if they were in any way real, might be demonic in nature. As for the claim that these manifestations were the dead returning to communicate with the living, 'he had special difficulty in believing that spiritual agents were likely to confine their operations to chairs and tables, badly spelt letters, and mawkish sentiments'. On the domestic front, his home had something of a supernatural reputation:

> Living in an old house, haunted, it was said, by the learned shade of George Buchanan, in which certainly the strangest and most unaccountable noises were frequently heard, his footsteps used sometimes to perform the transit from his study to his bedroom, in the dead of night, in double-quick time, and in the morning he used to confess that sitting up alone had made him feel quite 'eerie'.

On one occasion he had fled in terror because he had seen the figure of his friend the Revd Lyon 'rising up pale and grey, like a marble bust'. Charles Jobson Lyon (1789-1859) was an Episcopal clergyman and a distinguished historian of St Andrews. Brewster was greatly relieved to discover that, despite the vision, his friend was hale and well, while commenting that this then spoiled a rather good ghost story. You will notice that, as with the stories associated with Sharp and Ross, the figure seen here was the wraith or doppelganger of a living person, not the shade of someone deceased. Is this triple series of doppelgangers meaningful? Is there a connection to something in the environment of St Leonard's? Or is a pattern without significance? Once again, it is impossible to tell.

During Brewster's time, his neighbour in the larger building to the west, was Sir Hugh Lyon Playfair – the town's flamboyant Provost. After the latter's death in 1861, this western range was leased by the University as a residence for students, to be joined in 1863 by Brewster's house when the scientist moved on to become Principal of Edinburgh University. From then until 1882 – when the buildings were incorporated into the new St Leonard's

George Buchanan, Principal of St Leonard's College, and alleged ghost. (From A Biographical Dictionary of Eminent Scotsmen, *1855)*

School – the former Playfair and Brewster houses were home to around twenty-five University students per year. Among these residents was Andrew Lang, later to become one of the great St Andrews men of letters, and an author deeply interested in the supernatural and folklore. There are, however, no ghost stories from this period, or indeed ever since.

The Ghosts of Queen Mary's House

Although much altered, this house, fronting South Street, still retains its core original structure. In 1760, the house was let to Colonel John Nairne, who built a Gothic grotto in the garden between the house and St Leonard's Chapel to the south. At this point, the Chapel was roofless, and so the grotto – complete with a blazing fireplace and a series of niches filled with skulls – complemented the melancholy medieval ruins nicely. The grotto is sadly no more, but one of the skulls remained on its perch until 1927, when Queen Mary's House became the Library for St Leonard's School. Prior to this the house had been a private dwelling, and it is in this period that the ghost stories start – stories that have continued to the present day.

In 1977, Marjory Playfair-Hannay wrote a short piece called 'Recollections of "Queen Mary's"' for *Queen Mary's House and those who lived in it*, a booklet published by the Council of St Leonard's School. Ms Playfair-Hannay recalled that the house was occupied by a widow named Mrs Thomson, between 1902 and 1916, a period during which 'everyone recognized that there were many ghostly tales connected with Queen Mary's!' Sometime before the First World War, Mrs Thomson let the house out in August, and a family, complete with servants and copious baggage, moved in for their summer holiday. Within a week, however, they informed the agent that they could stay no longer, and, having paid the full month's rent, promptly decamped without further explanation. Mrs Thomson later met a fellow guest at a dinner party who knew the family concerned, and related what had happened. They had been in the ground-floor drawing-room after dinner when a tall, handsome man in Highland dress, emerged out of the full-length wall mirror and walked across the room and out of the door. The apparition looked neither to the left or right, and was silent throughout. By the following day, the tenants had given their notice to quit.

Mrs Thomson herself saw an apparition several times in one of the first floor rooms. The short, travel-stained man was in some distress and seemed to be trying to get at something, or into something, in the corner of the room. According to Ms. Playfair-Hannay, several other people also witnessed this figure.

In 1916, the house was bought by Captain Nunneley and his wife, both of whom made it very clear that they would have nothing to do with this nonsense about ghosts. However, when their daughter Catherine was three years old she was at her nursery window, which overlooked the garden to the south, and asked her nanny, 'Who is the funny old man in the brown dressing gown walking about in the garden reading a book?' According to the nanny, the little girl saw this figure more than once.

Sometime between 1916 and 1921, Marjory Playfair-Hannay stayed at the house when she was attending the Golf Ball, a social event held in September. On the first night, however, she went to a party elsewhere, and it was only on the second

Queen Mary's House from the south-east. (From MacGibbon and Ross, The castellated and domestic architecture of Scotland, *1887-92)*

Queen Mary's House, viewed from South Street. (Photo by Geoff Holder)

This room in Queen Mary's House is widely regarded as the dwelling of Mary, Queen of Scots. (Author's Collection)

evening that she met her two fellow guests: an Army officer from Yorkshire, and a young woman, neither of whom had visited St Andrews before. Just before 2 a.m., the three young people arrived home from the dance. Both women were staying on the top floor, and, before they retired, Ms Playfair-Hannay's neighbour mentioned that the previous night she had been woken at six in the morning by the sound of horses, jingling harnesses, and men shouting. The following day the Army officer told them that he had been in one of the rooms on the first floor as the clock struck 2 a.m. – and then heard, quite clearly, the tramp of feet and orders being given as if a guard was being changed. There was no stable near the house and, obviously, no night-watch. However, in another part of *Queen Mary's House and those who lived in it*, it is noted that a description of the property from 1785

includes the following element: 'that coach house belonging to the said house and situated between the road leading from the said Abbey Port to the Harbour of St Andrews and the Cathedral Church.'

Could there be some kind of ghostly connection between this eighteenth-century coach house and the sounds heard by the two young guests? And, speculating further, could these spectral sounds actually be the source for the occasional noises of hooves, rumbling wheels and jingling harnesses associated with Archbishop Sharp's phantom carriage? I have no idea, but the geography is right, and it remains an intriguing possibility.

Captain Nunneley died in 1921, and, five years later, his widow sold Queen Mary's House to St Leonard's School. In 1927 the school library was officially opened. But the ghosts had not gone away. The *Queen*

Mary's House booklet states that shortly after the school took over the building, the chairman of the school council, Bishop Plumb, undertook an exorcism throughout the entire house – complete with bell, book and candle – 'in order to ally fears among the girls'. This was presumably in 1927 or so, as Charles Edward Plumb, the fourth Bishop of St Andrews, Dunkeld and Dunblane, died in office in 1930.

After the Second World War, visiting American academic, Russell Kirk, investigated further for his book *St Andrews*. As a teacher at the school told him that, 'With the girls here, we *couldn't* have the ghost about,' this explains the exorcism that had to take place. From former pupils, Kirk learned that the two rooms of the library were 'haunted most disturbingly' by some unspecified, but awful, presence. In addition, many people had seen the figure of 'a little woman in dark clothing' hurrying out of the building into the garden. Leaving aside the change in gender, this diminutive apparition is reminiscent of the figures recorded in the early years of the century – the little man in dark or dirty clothing seen on the second floor, and the figure in a brown dressing gown spied in the garden. As far as Kirk's informants were concerned, the exorcism had cleared the library of these spirits.

In 2004, Carolyn Hilles – an academic from Rhode Island – penned an article entitled 'A Haunted School Library where Mary, Queen of Scots Slept' for the January issue of *Library Connection*, the newsletter of the Association of Independent School Librarians. The then librarian, Rona Wishart, and her assistant Stephanie Nicholson, described to Ms Hilles the ways in which the haunting continued in the building. The phenomena consisted of three kinds: auditory, such as the sound of footsteps; olfactory, with smells of antique perfumes or old wines wafting through the shelves; and physical.

The physical manifestations were by far the most striking. Light bulbs were commonly unscrewed from their sockets – on one occasion a student briefly stepped out of the library to ask a member of staff for help in finding a book. Coming back in, the pupil noticed that in the few seconds she had been outside, a light bulb had not only been unscrewed but had moved to the floor under a shelf. Electrical items were interfered with. A wall clock persistently stopped at 9.45, despite being declared in good working condition by a repairman. When, in an attempt to remove any possible vibration, the clock was bolted to the wall, the clock was found shattered. Doors opened of their own accord. Newspapers were scattered round when the building was empty. There was a distinct feeling that the phenomena got worse when someone in the building was in a mood or angry or boisterous. Carolyn Hilles claimed that many of the school's students, as well as the entire library staff, were thoroughly convinced of the reality of the haunting. Bringing the story up to 2011, Angela Tawse, the current librarian, told me that, despite working in the library everyday, often until quite late, she had never experienced any of the phenomena described above.

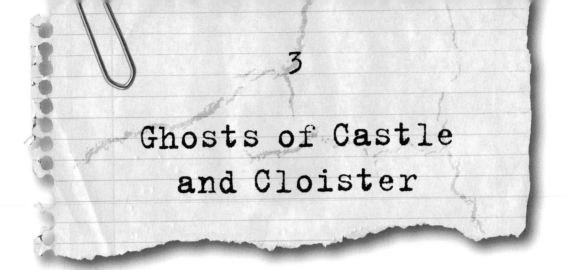

3

Ghosts of Castle and Cloister

Towers that the salt winds vainly beat.
Ghost-like and shadowy they stand
Dim mirrored in the wet sea-sand.

Andrew Lang, 'Almae Matres', 1890

The Ghosts of St Andrews Castle

Gaunt and weather swept, the ruins of the Castle of St Andrews stand on a cliff-edged outcrop jutting out to sea – a natural defensive position. The first castle was built here before 1200 AD, and the edifice was demolished, rebuilt, destroyed and rebuilt again several times in the thirteenth and fourteenth centuries. In the following century, the now completely-reconstructed castle became the palace residence of the Bishops and Archbishops of Scotland, and the occasional home of Scottish royalty. It also functioned as a state prison for everyone from common felons to aristocrats and other political prisoners, and the notorious escape-proof bottle-shaped dungeon, dug out of the very rock, can still be viewed in the remaining fragments of the Sea Tower. The courtyard, along with the front wall and gatehouse, still survive, but, over the

years, parts of the seaward walls, towers and other buildings have collapsed down the cliffs, and the site was used as a building quarry from 1654. It is a wonderfully atmospheric place to watch the rollers wash in from the grey North Sea, but visitors should be warned that it is very exposed to wind and rain.

The castle's most famous historical episode, a political assassination, is also the source of its most noted ghost. In the 1540s, Scotland was a snakepit, the usual jockeying for position by the competing noble families being exacerbated by a new factor – the religious Reformation. Scotland was resolutely Catholic, but politically and militarily weak, and both the two regional superpowers, Catholic France and Protestant England, were seeking to control Scotland via an arranged marriage with the infant Princess Mary Stuart (the future Mary, Queen of Scots). Opposing English intervention was a pro-French Catholic party led by Mary of Guise, the mother of the baby princess, and David Beaton, the Archbishop of St Andrews and a Cardinal of the Holy Roman Catholic Church. At the same time, individual Protestant preachers were travelling the

St Andrews Castle. Note the area in the foreground that fell into the sea, and the atmospheric fog rolling in. (Photo by Geoff Holder)

The drop into the notorious bottle dungeon of the castle. (Photo by Geoff Holder)

The execution of George Wishart. (From Foxe's Book of Martyrs, 1873)

reported to have watched the execution from a window in the castle. Wishart's initials are marked out in the road at the place of his death.

Brutality can kill one man but not a movement, and Beaton's treatment of Wishart made him a figure of hate for Protestant sympathisers. On 29 May 1546, three months after the martyrdom of George Wishart, a party gained access to the castle, murdered Beaton in his own apartments, and displayed his body from the castle walls. Suspended as it was by an arm and a leg, Beaton's naked and bloodied corpse was said to form the shape of a St Andrew's Cross. In an episode illustrative of how Beaton had raised hatred, as the corpse lay on the wallhead, one of the men in the castle urinated in the cardinal's mouth. One of the most widely-read works in Protestant England, John Foxe's *Actes and Monuments of these Latter and Perillous Days, Touching Matters of the Church* (usually known as *Foxe's Book of Martyrs*) described what happened next: 'And so like a butcher he lived, and like a butcher he died, and lay seven months and more unburied, and at last like a carrion was buried in a dunghill.' During these seven months, the corpse was kept preserved in salt, in a kist, held in the Sea Tower's prison.

The conspirators were prompted largely by personal enmity for the cardinal and a desire for revenge over the death of Wishart, but it is equally possible that they were acting, consciously or otherwise, as agents of Henry VIII of England, who had identified Beaton as a key obstacle to his plans for Scotland and the infant Mary Stuart. Certainly, when the conspirators then occupied the castle and defended it against a besieging force, they fully expected to be relieved by a naval force sent from England. This rescue fleet never sailed, largely

country, proclaiming the new Reformed religion. A number of these pioneers of the Reformation were prosecuted for heresy by the Catholic authorities, and burned at the stake. Cardinal Beaton, being the Pope's representative in Scotland, was duty-bound to pursue these 'heretics', and several were executed on his watch.

One of the most influential of these Protestant preachers was George Wishart. Having already escaped an assassination attempt by one of Beaton's men, Wishart was eventually captured, imprisoned in St Andrews, put on trial for heresy, and burned alive in front of the castle on 1 March 1546. The flames set off the bags of gunpowder strapped to Wishart, but the explosions did not kill him, merely prolonging his torment. Beaton was widely because as the siege proceeded, Henry VIII entered what was to be his terminal illness.

The year-long siege has bequeathed to us one of the most extraordinary pieces of military engineering in the world – the mine and countermine. The former is the tunnel the attackers dug to pass under the castle walls. It is wide and spacious, designed for the underground movement of pack animals and armed men. The countermine is the opposing tunnel constructed by the 'castilians', a narrow, twisting passage snaking through the rock, hastily constructed in a panic, with several

Part of the castle's subterranean siege tunnels. (Photo by Geoff Holder)

false starts. The two did meet up, wrecking the attackers' plans. The mine and countermine can be explored to this day – a highly recommended adventure, although not for those with claustrophobia. In 1931 James Wilkie, writing in *Bygone Fife from Culross to St Andrews*, claimed that a house in an unidentified narrow street near the castle was haunted by the sounds of armed conflict and apparitions of Highland clansmen and Hanoverian soldiers. If genuine, these phenomena were connected to the Jacobite period of the eighteenth century, and not to the siege of 1546.

In the end, it was a French fleet that arrived to break the siege, thus cementing a political alliance that saw Scotland become a client state of the Catholic superpower. The Protestants holed up in the castle could easily have been executed as rebels, but they received the comparatively light punishment of becoming galley slaves, rowing French warships. One of those consigned to this fate was one John Knox. In a later decade, Knox's passionate preaching would power the destructive tide of the Scottish Reformation, leading to the sacking of many of the religious buildings in St Andrews.

With spooky subterranean chambers and a history of violence, it is not surprising that the castle is supposed to be haunted. The ghost lore concentrates not on George Wishart, the Reformer ripped apart by gunpowder and flames, nor John Roger, another Protestant preacher who – whether by accident or design – died in the act of trying to escape from the castle's prison in 1544. Nor are apparitions reported of the many, but largely anonymous, men who died during the various assaults on the castle, or within the confines of the prison. Perhaps not surprisingly, the most noted phantom is the castle's chief celebrity,

Cardinal David Beaton, Archbishop of St Andrews, and rumored ghost. *(From* A Biographical Dictionary of Eminent Scotsmen, *1855)*

Archbishop David Beaton, who is seen gliding through the ruins in his distinctive red cardinal's robes and biretta headgear.

Or, at least, that's the story – and it is very much a story, with few actual reported sightings to back up the rumour, suggesting that the Cardinal is a folk ghost rather than a veritable apparition. In his two books, *The History of Fife* and *Bygone Fife from Culross to St Andrews*, James Wilkie stated that the ghost of the Cardinal had been seen both in the nineteenth century and after the First World War, but he gives no details as to when, or by whom, and the descriptions prove vague. Like others since, Wilkie states that the shade has been glimpsed in the gatehouse, looking out from the large empty window – his glance fixed on the spot where George Wishart met his martyrdom. It should be pointed out that the window thus referred to – indeed, the entire façade in which it sits – was built *after* Cardinal Beaton was murdered.

Wilkie does describe two witnessed apparitions. The first was seen by an anonymous visitor between one and two p.m. on a wet day, some time in the 1920s. An older woman in clothes from a vanished age walked across the courtyard from the gatehouse, passed the well, and then carried on right through the sea rail, 'turning to her left where no foot can now tread'. In other words, she was walking in mid-air in the part of the castle that has long collapsed into the sea. In the second case, a woman watched as a handsome 'foreign-looking girl' talked excitedly to a man in 'fancy dress' in South Street, then a dwarf ran up to them and the lady burst into tears. Later research came up with the historical titbit that the news of Cardinal Beaton's murder was apparently broken to a fair Spanish lady by a dwarf.

However, we do have a more recent report that might point to the ghostly cardinal's existence. In November 1978, Helen Cook wrote an article on 'Haunted St Andrews' for *The Scots Magazine*. Dick Martin, the then Castle Custodian, told her about a recent incident. A school party had visited under the guidance of a teacher, who happened to be a former student at St Andrews. Revisiting his youth, he and a friend returned after hours and attempted to enter the castle surreptitiously. As they climbed the fence, the teacher saw a shadowy figure moving from one window to another in the south-facing gatehouse. It could have been a flesh-and-blood human being – except that there had been no floors at this level since the castle was abandoned in the seventeenth century. There is nothing in this sighting to specifically link it with Beaton, and the figure could have been created by an optical effect, perhaps a car headlight or a curtain closing in one of the houses opposite. But the episode is intriguing, even suggestive – although I do suspect that 'Cardinal Beaton' is more a ghost of folklore rather than actual, true-life sightings.

The Cardinal's ghost has, however, made two definitive appearances in literature. In 1547, just months after his death, Beaton's shade was the principal character in 'The Tragedie of the Cardinall', a poem by the courtier and intellectual-about-town Sir David Lyndsay. In the poem, the Cardinal returns from the dead to advise both kings and priests that advancement in the church should be based on merit, not on corrupt practices or on personal connections. Beaton's ghost admits that he became Archbishop through greed and dodgy dealing – and points out where *that* got him. Then, in 1902, Robert Marshall published *The Haunted Major*, a golfing farce that resembles – and may have influenced – the Jeeves and Wooster novels of P.G. Wodehouse. The story concerns Major the Honourable John William Wentworth Gore, an insufferable sporting bore. In pursuit of a rich widow, Gore accepts a challenge on the St Andrews Links – despite never having played golf before. It is only with the assistance of the ghost of Cardinal Beaton – or Smeaton as he is rendered here – that the Major triumphs. Despite its prehistoric class attitudes, the novel is genuinely funny, and is the only book about golf that I am ever likely to read.

Helen Cook's 1978 article also included a sighting of a ghostly celebrity from the opposite side of the religious divide. Sometime in the early 1960s, Priscilla Robertson was taking an evening walk with her fiancé beside the castle when she saw the apparition of John Knox. Knox was standing, watching the castle intently. Unlike most representations of Knox, which show him as the greybearded firebrand of later life, this was a well-dressed younger man, wearing a skull-cap and a long, dark, cloak-like garment. His facial hair was trimmed into a very short pointed beard. At the time, Priscilla Robertson did not realise who it was, but later she read an illustrated biography of Knox and recognised him from an illustration of the preacher as a young man. When her fiancé switched on a torch to illuminate the shadows, the figure vanished.

Helen Cook also mentioned an earlier, but undated, sighting of Knox, when an unnamed lecturer at the University encountered his apparition at one a.m. in a moonlit North Street, close to St Salvator's Chapel. This version of Knox was stern, elderly, long-bearded and dressed in a long Geneva gown with clerical markings. He was accompanied by a second apparition,

John Knox, Protestant Reformer, and alleged ghost. (From The Scottish Nation, *1877)*

that of an armed man with a metal helmet. Later research uncovered the fact that when the older Knox walked abroad in St Andrews, he was escorted by a member of the town guard.

The Monkish Ghosts of St Andrews Cathedral and St Rule's Tower

Ghosts of monks are always popular, perhaps because the robe and hood gives them an added air of mystery, and there is something about identifying a spectre as a man of God that adds an extra *frisson* to the experience.

St Andrews has enough reports of phantom monks to fill a chapter house. James Wilkie, for example, describes how a 'lady of position in the county' rented a large but unidentified house in the old part of St Andrews. One night, before the new moon, she awoke to find the bedroom, quite bizarrely, flooded with moonlight. Standing in the beams pouring through the window was a solitary monk. Once she switched on the electric light, both the monk and the eerie moonlight vanished. But when she turned off her own light, both the monk and the lunar glow reappeared. Making enquiries with her landlady the following day, the witness at first received evasive replies, but her persistence eventually uncovered the fact that the ghostly monk had been sighted on several previous occasions. According to Wilkie, 'An undertaking was given that the house should not be identified, lest the story interfere with the letting of the rooms.' At a later date, a lady opened a door in the same house to find four monks seated and standing around the fireplace. 'She was accustomed to abnormal experiences,'

All that remains of Blackfriars Chapel, destroyed in the Reformation of 1559. (Photo by Geoff Holder)

Above *A simulacrum of what is supposed to be the scorched face of the executed martyr Patrick Hamilton, in the tower of St Salvator's Chapel. (Photo by Geoff Holder)*

Left *Studentlore has it that stepping on these initials of Patrick Hamilton, marked in the cobbles at St Salvator's, will result in the failure of exams. (Photo by Geoff Holder)*

writes Wilkie intriguingly, 'and, after contemplating the scene, quietly withdrew'.

Elsewhere, Helen Cook, in *A Haunting of Ghosts,* retells the traditional story of the Dominican monk Alexander Campbell, who supposedly haunts the ruined fragment of Blackfriars' Chapel on South Street. According to the standard tale, his spectre is condemned to walk the earth because he was partly responsible for the burning at the stake of the Protestant reformer Patrick Hamilton in 1527. The church of the Black Friars was destroyed in 1559. Also annihilated in the same year was the Franciscan friary that once stood off Greyfriars Garden (the current Student Union building probably stands on the site of the friary church). Here, the apparition of the monk is headless, and once again, according to tradition, continues to tread the grounds of his former monastic home in penance for a terrible crime.

Far more attention, however, is focused on the ghost of Thomas Plater. Any website or journalistic feature on the hauntings of St Andrews will include this story of the monk who murdered his superior, and then haunted the cathedral until his bones were reburied; and the associated tale of the kindly ghost of the victim, who assists visitors climbing the many stairs of St Rule's Tower. As is typically the case, these stories have usually been shorn of their sources and checkable details; here, for the first time in print for more than a century, I have brought together all the available documentation on the murder of Prior Robert Montrose by the monk Thomas Plater, and the sightings of their respective apparitions.

The eastern headland at St Andrews has been a Christian sacred site since the Dark Ages. A monastic community was established there by at least 747 AD, if not earlier. By the tenth century, St Andrews

The gaunt St Rule's Tower, the last remnant of St Rule's Church. (Ségolène Dupuy)

– but the story suited the propaganda needs of the early Scottish church, and once St Andrew was declared the patron saint of Scotland, the newly-renamed town of St Andrews became a major pilgrimage site. Pilgrims brought wealth and prestige, and soon the monks were embarking on their first cathedral.

The Cathedral Church of St Rule was probably built between 1127-1150 AD. Small by the standards of the grandiose European cathedrals, it was nonetheless one of the largest structures in Scotland at the time. St Rule's has now almost entirely disappeared, with the notable exception of the great square tower. Even without its spire, the tower dominates the area and its simple style of architecture only serves to reinforce its air of great antiquity. The tower's architectural neighbour is its successor, the vast cathedral – begun about 1160 AD. The longest building in medieval Scotland, the new cathedral was composed of two principal parts – the enormous church, and the priory, the home of the Augustinian Canons who served the cathedral. The head of the community was the Bishop, usually a skilled politician deeply involved in the government of the day; for this reason, the day-to-day running of the priory was down to a Prior. In 1559, the cathedral was ransacked of its furnishings and treasures by a Reformation mob incited by John Knox. The great church was abandoned and within a short time the roof was stripped for its lead, and the high-quality stone of the immense edifice was being quarried for building projects elsewhere. By 1597 the site was already on the way to ruination.

From 1385 the Prior had been Robert de Montrose. Walter Bower, writing in one of the earliest chronicles of Scottish history, the *Scotichronicon,* eulogised the Prior in the most saintly of terms:

had become the centre of the Scottish Church, as the former headquarters at Iona, on the west coast, was now too vulnerable to Viking raids. The Fife community was initially known as Kilrimont, but the name soon changed to St Andrews because the early abbey supposedly held the most important relics in Scottish Christendom – the bones of St Andrew, one of the apostles of Jesus. In a masterful mix of mythmaking and fiction, a legend had grown up that a Mediterranean priest named St Rule, had transferred the sacred relics from Greece to Fife in the fourth century after Christ. If there were indeed any of St Andrew's bones in the Scottish shrine, they would have actually been brought from Rome by an Anglo-Saxon bishop some 400 years later

The east gable of the Cathedral, and St Rule's Tower. (Ségolène Dupuy)

The ruined Cathedral from the west. (Ségolène Dupuy)

He was a man of great knowledge and eloquence, and a distinguished Preacher, an upholder of the ancient Discipline, a pattern to the Flock in the Monastery, and a good Shepherd to the people; for he did not despise the people, but instructed them, and rendered to every one his due. He did not flatter the great, nor fear their threats; he did not oppress the poor, but protected them. The errors of those subject to him he did not overlook, but corrected; in all things showing himself respectful to his seniors, mild to his juniors, gentle to his Religious Brethren, unyielding to the proud and obstinate, condescending to the humble, and tender-hearted to the penitent.

It is thanks to Bower's *Scotichronicon* (completed in the 1440s), and another early work, *The Chronicle of John Law*, written in St Andrews around 1521, that we know all that we do about the murder of Robert de Montrose. Everything else written afterwards is merely unsupported storytelling. Both Bower and Law tell us that one of the canons, a Thomas Plater (or Platar, or Platter), deeply resented the discipline imposed upon him by the Prior. Bower calls Plater a monk, while Law promotes him to sub-prior. Both, however, agree what happened in 1393. In Bower's words:

One evening when the Prior was alone, and was going up, as usual, from the Cloister to the Dormitory for the night, Plater, watching his opportunity, attacked him, and, drawing an iron dagger from under his cloak, mortally wounded him.

Robert de Montrose survived for three days before expiring of his wound. He was buried in the Chapter House of the Priory. Plater tried to make his escape but was quickly caught. Two days after Montrose's funeral, the murderer was tried in an ecclesiastical court headed by the Bishop, Walter Trail, and condemned to perpetual imprisonment. Bower then gives us Plater's fate: 'Partaking scantily of the bread of grief and the water of affliction, he soon died, and was buried in a dunghill'. This, then, is all we know about Prior Montrose and the monk who murdered him. Which brings us on to the stories of their ghosts. It is not clear how long a story has been circulating that the spirit of Robert de Montrose could be seen in St Rule's Tower. Either William Linskill already knew the tale, or he embellished it, for, as might be expected, it appears in *St Andrews Ghost Stories*. According to Linskill, the prior's ghost could often be seen peeping over the parapet, and then falling – or jumping – from the tower. In this version – a complete contradiction of the historical account – the murder took place within the tower, with Plater stabbing his superior on the ladder leading to the top, then throwing the body off. I very much doubt that anyone falling 110ft would still be alive, never mind survive for three days, as happened to Montrose. Other fantasies from the Linskill account include more detail on Plater's sins, such as playing practical jokes and trying to seduce the lady-in-waiting of the wife of Earl Douglas, and the statement that the murder took place on a moonlit night just before Christmas (none of these details are in the original accounts).

To be fair, Linskill claimed he obtained this information from yet another one of his garrulous ghost-hunting acquaintances, a Captain Chester. Chester, who was probably as fictional as his tale, described seeing a figure fall from the summit of St Rule's, and then, a few minutes later, passing a monk dressed in the Augustinian habit.

The night stair of the Priory, where Thomas Plater murdered Prior Robert de Montrose in 1393. (Photo by Geoff Holder)

Later that night, the spirit visited Chester in his bedroom; he introduced himself as Prior Robert of Montrose and then passed over the very dagger that had killed him all the centuries ago. It should be noted that modern accounts of the ghost in the tower tend to omit this bedchamber episode, no doubt because it seems too far-fetched, even for contemporary ghost-fanciers. I also point out that Montrose's reported speech is suspiciously couched in the style of an educated Edwardian gentleman, and not Latin or impenetrable medieval Scots, the languages he would have used in life.

The ghost of Prior Montrose is associated not with the stair to the dormitory – which is where he was stabbed – nor with the chapter house, the location of his grave. In normal circumstances, I would suggest that St Rule's Tower has been chosen as the location by the mechanics of telling a good story – neither the stair nor the chap-ter house have any substantial or obvious remains, while the tower is both conveniently close and undeniably dramatic. A ghost falling off a tall tower is a better story than an apparition on a few dull nondescript stones.

But then we have the testimony of Michael Elder, interviewed by author Helen Cook for her 1983 book *A Haunting of Ghosts*. Ascending St Rule's has been a popular pursuit for decades, and is something I recommend to everyone (as long as you can cope with a narrow spiral staircase and a lung-busting number of steps). On a bright Thursday afternoon in August 1946, Mr Elder undertook the climb, and just before the top – where he stumbled up a section in complete darkness – he turned a corner and saw a dark figure. The man was illuminated only from the waist down, the light from the narrow window leaving his upper body and face in darkness. He was wearing a cassock

The spiral staircase of St Rule's Tower. The alleged ghost of a monk was encountered here in 1946. (Photo by Geoff Holder)

tied by a girdle at the waist, and said: 'It's all right, you may hold on to me, if you want to.' Mr Elder politely declined and carried on to the top, where he admired the sunlit panorama and chatted briefly with another visitor. At this point he thought just how odd it was that he had passed a monk on the stairs, so he hurried back down. The rest of the tower was deserted – and there was no hiding place – and when he emerged from the ground floor door he saw the cathedral custodian speaking to two men cutting the grass at the foot of the tower. All three had been there when Mr Elder arrived, and they had seen no-one emerge from the single entrance/exit in the intervening minutes. None of them had seen the monk enter, and the custodian was there to collect tickets from visitors.

Of course, there is absolutely nothing to suggest that this kindly apparition was indeed Robert de Montrose. It is only the murder, and the subsequent fame of killer and victim in print, that links the two in the mind. Dozens of monks must have died in the Priory, and many of their stone-cut graves, complete with a carved niche for the head, can still be seen among the ruins. But these men are unknown except to a few specialists, and so we assume that the monk of St Rule's *must* be Robert de Montrose, simply because his murder lifts him above the parapet of history. Once again, celebrity culture triumphs in ghost land.

As for Thomas Plater, the story of his ghost is even more intriguing. Supposedly the 'wicked monk' was often seen in the cathedral grounds in the nineteenth century, although the only actual account that I can track down is in *Bygone Fife from Culross to St Andrews* by James Wilkie. A well-known local woman saw the face of a man looking out of a window in one of the ruined towers. Needless to say, there are no stairs to these gaunt windows. The apparition took place at 2.30 p.m. on a summer's afternoon, and the witness described the man as aged between forty and fifty, 'but with a face that seemed younger'. Once again, there is no obvious identifier in this description – it is the witness who made the bridge between the apparition she glimpsed and the historical Thomas Plater, simply because she had heard of the murder.

Be that as it may, things took a definite turn for the bizarre in 1898. The events were first briefly documented by David Hay Fleming, in the *St Andrews Citizen* on 24 September 1898, and expanded in 1931 in *Bygone Fife from Culross to St Andrews*, where James Wilkie drew on unpublished correspondence from both Dr Hay Fleming and Mrs Thomson, the former occupant of Queen Mary's House (*see* Chapter 2). In the 1890s, parts of the Priory had been the subject of an archaeological dig (the reconstructed sections from this dig can today be identified by the dark red stone deliberately used as a contrast to the grey of the medieval stonework). The instigator of the excavation was John Patrick Crichton-Stuart, third Marquess of Bute. Lord Bute was an extraordinary character – a mystical Roman Catholic, an active member of the Society for Psychical Research, a builder of fantasy castles (such as Cardiff Castle and Castell Coch in Wales, and Mount Stuart on the Isle of Bute), and a wealthy romantic

antiquarian fascinated by the Middle Ages and questions of life after death.

During the dig several skeletons were discovered and subsequently reburied. Shortly afterwards, a billiard-marker at one of the St Andrews hotels woke up to find the apparition of a monk at his bedside. He was wearing what was later identified as a penitent's robe. The figure faded away after a few moments, but returned several days later, this time delivering a spoken message – he said that he was the shade of Thomas Plater, and that the work in the priory had disturbed his remains. As he had never received Christian burial – remember, the medieval chroniclers stated he had been disposed of in a dunghill – Plater now asked that a request be made to Lord Bute for a proper burial service. The billiard-marker, a pious Catholic, told his brother, one of the masons on the project, about the visitation. The mason passed the ghostly message up the line, and eventually it reached the ears of Lord Bute.

What happened next is a tribute both to Bute's power and influence, and to the depth of his religious beliefs. One of the skeletons was immediately exhumed. On 15 July 1898, the bones were wrapped in the habit of an Augustinian monk, complete with a metal cross, and a rosary, and taken to one of the vaults within the priory, where, at a temporary altar, a mass was said for the repose of the soul of Thomas Plater. The officiating priest was the Revd Sir David Hunter Blair, a well-connected Benedictine monk and the translator from German of *A History of the Catholic Church in Scotland*. Accompanied by Lord Bute and the billiard-marker, the skeleton was then laid to rest in consecrated ground within the cathedral burying-ground, with the last rites being performed by another monk. Sadly I have been unable to locate this gravesite, which was apparently to the south of St Rule's Tower. Linskill, to his credit, found the entire episode ludicrous, and told H. V. Morton that he had heard the billiard-marker emigrated to Australia to get away from the ghost.

What are we to make of all this? Hay Fleming pointed out that he had mentioned the murder to the masons sometime *before* Plater appeared to the hotel worker. Did the story get around, excite the imagination of a particularly religious individual, and hence create a ghost story out of nothing? Or did it all really happen as described? Certainly Lord Bute believed the story, as the elaborate arrangements for the funeral demonstrate. But were the re-interred bones really those of Thomas Plater? (Dr Hay Fleming was adamant that the original burial site 'was certainly no midden'). The episode echoes with these niggling doubts, but as there appear to have been no reliable sightings of the 'wicked monk' in the twentieth century, perhaps Thomas Plater – murderer – was indeed finally laid to rest in 1898.

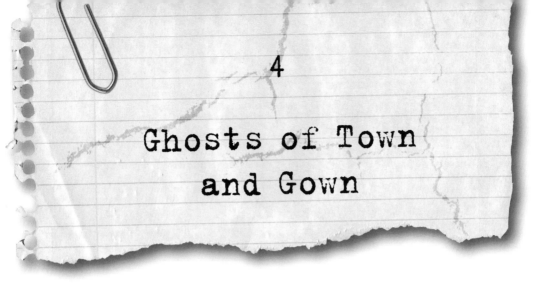

4

Ghosts of Town and Gown

My thoughts are with the Dead; with them
I live in long-past years,
Their virtues love, their faults condemn,
Partake their hopes and fears;
And from their lessons seek and find
Instruction with an humble mind

Robert Southey, 'My Days Among
the Dead are Passed', 1818

A Haunted Theatre

One of the more common practices in ghostology is the tendency to personalise ghosts. People who regularly encounter an apparition sometimes like to name the spirit – 'Jack/Jock', 'Janet', 'John', and 'Elsie/Elspeth' are all frequently found in the literature. This is not to say that these are the genuine names of any once-alive individual – just that it is in human nature to impose a sense of a personalised individual onto otherwise nameless phantoms. At times, a ghost is granted an honorific – the name of a specific, usually well-known person, even if there is absolutely no overt connection between the phenomena and the name. This is what happens when ghosts get identified, without any good reason, as Mary, Queen of Scots or Bonnie Prince Charlie. A more local example can be found in the Byre Theatre, where the once-resident ghost was universally known as 'Chas', after Charles Marford, the theatre's dynamic director during the Second World War.

The Byre has had three distinct phases during its distinguished life. The original Byre Theatre, or Byre 1 as it is called, was founded in 1933, in a former cowshed reached through a pend off Abbey Street. The guiding light was local journalist and man of letters, Alexander B. Paterson. The first play was performed in 1935, and, with limited resources but boundless resourcefulness, the theatre became an established and much-loved fixture in St Andrews. In 1970 the brand new Byre Theatre, or Byre 2, opened a few hundred yards to the north. Byre 3, the current incarnation, opened its doors in 2001 on the same spot as Byre 2, and remains as popular as ever.

In the spring of 1940, the St Andrews Repertory Company, beset by wartime restrictions and loss of personnel to the call-up, found their saving light in the form of Charles 'Chas' Marford, the former stage manager of the Old Vic Theatre in London.

The entrance of the current Byre Theatre ('Byre 3').
(Photo by Geoff Holder)

you could hear a seat tip up by itself. Sometimes this could cause a hesitation in the performance as the actors strained to look into the gloom to see if there had been anyone in the seat or not. If there was no sign of anyone it was said that Charles Marford was commenting on the quality of the play. The seats in Byre 2 had a very distinctive metallic sound when they tipped so you couldn't mistake the noise for anything else.

During the war years, Marford, and his wife Molly Tapper, kept the beleaguered Byre open, with Marford taking on the roles of sound and light technicians, stage manager and actor – all in the same show. Marford died in 1955. It is not clear when the 'hauntings' started, but very quickly the ghost was dubbed 'Chas'. When the new theatre (Byre 2) opened in 1970, the phenomena relocated to the modern building along with the actors. Helen Cook, in her 1983 book *A Haunting of Ghosts*, states that the incidents only started in Byre 2 when a bust of Shakespeare was rather belatedly transferred from Byre 1.

No-one at the theatre can now remember what happened to that Shakespearean bust, but there are memories a-plenty of the incidents in Byre 2. In November 2011, Alan Tricker, who has been involved with the Byre since 1975, was kind enough to share his recollections with me:

It was a common story in Byre 2 that the ghost of Charles Marford used to watch the dress rehearsals of plays and make his views known on the quality of the performance. Sometimes during the dress

Alan also remembered that off-stage, actors were always warned not to use the loo during a performance, because the waste pipe from the dressing rooms descended behind the stage – and the flush of water could be heard from the audience. One Sunday evening, during a rehearsal, the toilet flushed. Which was strange, seeing as the only people in the theatre that night were all on stage. An actor went upstairs and checked both dressing rooms and the Green Room, all of which were empty – and no-one could have come down the stairs without being noticed. The company became frightened, the rehearsal fell apart, and pretty soon everyone just packed up and went home early. On another occasion, Alan was alone on Byre 2, having just finished painting the stage and clearing up. As he went to the back door to set the alarm he had the distinct sensation of someone standing right behind him – but when he turned, the space was empty. He exited with speed and felt relieved to be standing outside on Abbey Street.

Another Byre regular told me that everyone was of the opinion that the 'ghost' appeared as a chilly presence on the long stairway between the stage and the Green Room. If you encountered a spot where the temperature dropped suddenly, it was prudent to step aside to let 'Chas' past. Helen

Cook's book added some more details: electrical switches would turn on and off for no reason, inexplicable noises would be heard, and the frequency of the noises would increase if rehearsals were not going well, as if the 'ghost' was expressing its frustration. On one occasion a tape of sound effects was cued in the middle of a play, as usual, but what was heard by the actors and audience was the sound of unknown music. When the play was over the offending tape was played again to identify the problem – but only the scheduled sounds were heard, and not the inexplicable music.

Of course, it is possible to attribute at least some of incidents to mundane physical events, such as fluctuations in temperature caused by environmental factors in the fabric of the building, along with mechanical malfunction, human error and the sense of 'eerie expectation' that can exist in the empty and semi-darkened spaces of a theatre. We will never know whether the ghost dubbed 'Chas' ever did walk the boards in Byre 1 and Byre 2, as, since Byre 3 opened in 2001, there have been no tales of mysterious manifestations or interrupted rehearsals.

A Ghost Outside the Byre

When Byre 2 was built in 1970, it was linked to South Street and Abbey Walk by a newly-created pedestrian north/south route through a small pend and the courtyard of South Court. This thoroughfare, still popular, passes through the 'lang riggs' or gardens of the restored medieval buildings that surround this secluded public space. It was in this charming spot that an American couple, on a golfing holiday in 1973, both clearly saw an apparition from another age. They related their experience

The medieval pend leading into South Court and The Byre. (Photo by Geoff Holder)

to local author Raymond Lamont-Brown, who included it in his 1978 book *Phantoms of the Theatre*. At first they suspected nothing was amiss, as they thought they were seeing an actor, dressed in leather boots, tight trousers and a white shirt with a frilly frontage, standing outside the theatre entrance and reading the poster of forthcoming events. Mr Herman Josephson took a few photographs of the actor in his costume, and clearly saw the man through the viewfinder.

At this point the couple moved closer – and noticed that the figure was semi-transparent – they could see right through him. Mrs Josephson felt ill at the sight, and had to sit down on a nearby bench. When they looked back, the man had disappeared. Later, when the film was developed, there was no sign of the apparition on the photographs.

University Ghosts

The University of St Andrews was founded in 1413, making it the third oldest university in the UK, after Oxford and Cambridge.

St Salvator's. (From Charles Rogers, History of St Andrews, *1849)*

Like its English cousins and peers, it was collegiate in structure; St Salvator's College was founded in 1450, St Leonard's College in 1512, and St Mary's College in 1538. In the eighteenth century, St Salvator's and St Leonard's amalgamated to form United College, whose campus was at St Salvator's; over the years the names 'St Leonard's' and 'United College' have faded away, leaving the principal medieval colleges as St Mary's (on South Street) and St Salvator's (on North Street). Both have charming quadrangles bounded by significant architecture from various eras. Expansion over the past century and a half means that the University buildings are now threaded through virtually every district of St Andrews, with major modern extensions to the west of the confines of the old town.

In 1728, a William Douglass described St Salvator's: 'The common hall and schools are vastly large; and the cloisters and private lodgings for masters and scholars have been very magnificent and convenient.' By the early nineteenth century, decay had set in – R.G. Cant's 1992 history of the University, quotes official opinions about the state of the buildings at United College: part was 'entirely ruinous and incapable of repair'; the classrooms were 'extremely mean, small, confined, and insufficient'; and the north block facing the quadrangle was 'in a most dilapidated state'. In 1829-31 the east block was demolished and replaced, and a similar fate overtook the arcaded north block in 1845-46. Up to this point the buildings at St Salvator's/United College had provided both classrooms for teaching, and rooms for student accommodation, but after the refurbishments the college became entirely academic, and the students moved out to purpose-built halls of residence elsewhere.

In 1875, Revd James W. Taylor, Free Church Minister of Flisk in north Fife, published his book *Historical Antiquities of Fife*. It contains a particularly interesting aside about the pre-refurbishment United College:

> Let us try and recall the appearance of that old College Court of St Salvator, as it looked thirty years ago. Dingy and decaying and old-world-like it seemed, but it was full of interest. On its east and south sides were the ruins of the houses in which the College bread was baked, and the brewery. Along the north side extended a range of barrack-like building, supplying in its upper stories rooms for the collegians, and from which the last occupant was driven by the nightly invasion of a ghost.

Unfortunately, Revd Taylor tells us nothing more about this nightly visitation on the 1840s, and none of the other histories or reminiscences of the University from this period mention it. So we are left with just this single sentence to pique our interest – and nothing more.

In November 2009, *The StAndard*, the magazine for University staff, revealed that Castlecliffe, one of the grand cliff top buildings on The Scores, also had a tale of ghostly manifestation. Castlecliffe was built in 1869 as a residence for Professor Thomas Purdie. In later years it became, successively, an auxiliary hospital during the First World War, and then a girls' boarding school. Although it is currently occupied by the School of Economics, for many years the mansion was home to the Department of Spanish, and it is to this period that the ghost story belongs. Philippa Dunn's article uncovered the story of a student who saw the apparition of a soldier dressed in a uniform of the First World War. The figure was waiting nonchalantly outside the door to the office of the Head of the School of Hispanic Languages, which is now the main office of the School of Economics. The soldier vanished before the student's eyes,

United College, after the renovations of 1845-46 had removed the ghost. (From Charles Rogers, History of St Andrews, *1849)*

and apparently his ghost was seen by other witnesses at later dates, although we have no details. Many years later, a groundsman at the adjacent St Andrews Castle told the staff at the School of Economics that the ghost was the spirit of a soldier who had returned from the trenches with a Victoria Cross. The local hero had apparently been killed sometime in the 1930s while cleaning the windows of Castlecliffe.

Further investigation unearthed an identity for this individual: Corporal (later Sergeant) John Ripley of the first battalion of the Black Watch. On 9 May 1915 his conspicuous bravery during an engagement at the Rue du Bois, left him with severe head wounds, and the highest military honour that could be awarded to anyone in the British armed forces. At forty-seven years of age, he was one of the oldest recipients of the VC. On 24 October 2001, *Fife Today* published an article on the ceremony that commemorated the refurbishment of Sgt Ripley's grave at Largo Cemetery, in Upper Largo. According to the piece, once Ripley returned from France he lived in St Andrews, working as a chimney sweep and slater, and serving in the town's fire brigade. He died on 14 August 1933, after falling from a ladder; he was 66.

On the face of it, this seems to be a plausible connection. The apparition was a First World War soldier; and John Ripley was a hero of that war who lived and died in St Andrews. However, as usual, I am not entirely convinced. In 1917 Castlecliffe was operating as an Auxiliary Hospital under the Scottish Command arm of the military; dozens of wounded soldiers would have come and gone, and I have no doubt some lounged nonchalantly outside an office door. I suspect that John Ripley's local fame – he was not just a war hero, but a war hero with a VC – has inflected the ghost story.

That is, it is his celebrity that drives the story, not a positive identification between man and phantom. It is not clear where his fatal accident took place – it could have been at Castlecliffe, or it could have been somewhere else. If the sighting of the apparition is genuine, then it is likely to be connected to an anonymous wounded soldier recovering at the hospital. This may make for a less dramatic and satisfying narrative, but then ghost stories should not really be about the power of celebrity.

Undergraduate Terrors

Over two separate periods, in August 2003 and January to July 2005, the messageboards on the St Andrews student-run website The Sinner, ran hot with posts describing ghosts and rumours of ghosts. Most first-year students live in halls, and many continue to do so in subsequent years, so, not surprisingly, many of the online conversations dealt with halls of residence, and proved to be a veritable smorgasbord of what might be described as a subset of the urban legend phenomenon, something we might call 'undergraduate legend'.

The hall most mentioned in the posts was McIntosh Hall, also known as Chattan, because it incorporates the former hotel Chattan House. First acquired by the University (in part) in 1921, it took on its current form in 1939, and is a grand structure stretching the length of Abbotsford Crescent, with around 200 students occupying five floors. Several of those posting passed on what were clearly the two principal legends of the hall: that a fire on the upper floor had killed several people, and that a male student had died when falling out of a fourth floor window (which supposedly happened on the first day of term,

The Golf Links. Hamilton Hall is the tall building in the centre. (From E.S. Valentine, Fifeshire, 1910)

or the last day of term, or the student holiday of Raisin Day, or one of several other days). These two legends – for legends they are, with no records of such deaths – provide the alleged reason for the ghosts who supposedly haunt the hall. The fire story seems to have grown from puzzlement over the fact that some isolated rooms on the top floor are blocked off. These rooms once belonged to the warden, and were closed off after a minor incident showed that there was no viable fire exit.

Rumours aside, a few of the students reported what they claimed to be genuine experiences. On 23 June 2005, 'ariel' described seeing a black figure walking past her bed in her room on D floor (the ground floor). She also reported a persistent sense of presence in the room, as if someone was standing by her bed. Three days later 'Kate Bush' replied with an experience from C floor (the first floor), although her description merely said it was similar to the events described by 'ariel'. The student was so scared that she had a friend come

round to pray with her through the night. In a different post (26 January 2005) 'Kate Bush' also mentioned that she had glimpsed an apparition in the common room, while on the same day 'Beckie' stated that a friend of hers had seen 'something' in one of the shared bathrooms on D floor, while she herself reported a sense of presence in her bedroom. Meanwhile, 'tylermatts' (7 July 2005) talked of seeing lights on in the windows of the closed off and abandoned rooms, and passed on a story from a former resident of the top floor (A floor) who often heard footsteps running down the hall into the closed off area. And, on 18 August 2003, 'diddy reese' reported the experiences of both himself and several other students, each of whom had been alone in the common room when they heard 'five quick, random notes' played out on the piano there. The general explanation was mice running over the strings, but the effect was eerie.

The stories relating to the former Hamilton Hall, on Golf Place, were very similar. Built in 1895 as the Grand Hotel, the iconic building dominates the view from the Links, and hence is frequently seen in television coverage of the Open. It also featured in the film *Chariots of Fire*. Hamilton Hall was a hall of residence from the 1940s until 2006, when the building was sold for private development. The most common tale circulating around the student residents was that the top storey was haunted by the ghosts of two people who had died in a fire there. Access to the sixth floor was indeed barred, and the route to the warning sign forbidding entry was up a pair of metal stairs, which was an unsettling climb – the perfect introduction to the 'environment of anxiety', which is such a fertile ground for imaginative fears. And there was indeed a fire on the top floor in the 1970s, damaging two small rooms. No-one, however, was hurt, never mind killed. It is another example of the trope known as 'this building is haunted by those who died in a fire', a piece of undergraduate folklore that has become attached to many of the halls of residence.

Rather more interesting were fragments of episodes related to the fourth floor at Hamilton. On 31 January 2005, 'raheli' stated that the hall manageress had a file of sightings stretching back fifteen years, with several students independently providing sketches of the same bearded male figure. Without further knowledge it is impossible to draw any conclusions about these reports, for once again they may be products of life in a grandiose Victorian building. On 18 August 2003, for example, 'diddy reese' stated that, even though he had experienced nothing in the way of phenomena, his brief stay on the fourth floor the previous summer had convinced him that Hamilton Hall was 'the single creepiest place in St Andrews'.

David Russell Hall (or DRH) was a 1960s-built hall that has now been demolished and replaced with the David Russell Apartments complex on Buchanan Gardens. On 24 June 2005, 'windowcandy' recalled some strange experiences in the block known as DRH Tulloch a few years previously. Steam from a bath would form a human face before dissipating, while running water and the sound of splashing was heard from an empty bathroom. Meanwhile, on 27 June 2005, 'harmless loony' reported that each night a male figure with a 'dark aura' would walk into a bedroom in New Hall and sit on the bed. New Hall, part of the modern University complex on the North Haugh, was built in 1993. The student said that two friends had also seen the figure and were scared to enter the room, and eventually 'harmless loony' got rid of the presence through the use of prayer.

Outside the halls of residence, rented flats came in for some ghostly speculation. On 26 January 2005, 'sweet' considered that the garden of "a cold, dark, draughty" flat on Hope Street was haunted by the ghost of an old lady watering the plants. Meanwhile 'ariel' (27 June 2005) claimed to have seen a spectral figure in a long black coat walking along Hope Street, and on 26 January 2005, 'Guest' stated that a kind of poltergeist was operating in a house down Gillespie Wynd, off The Scores. Another minor bout of poltergeist activity was claimed for a flat in Melbourne Place, while a figure was glimpsed by two people in another flat in College Street – both these incidents were mentioned by 'Dave' on 18 August 2003. Further afield, 'warrengato' (28 January 2005) reported sightings of mysterious candle-like lights on the beach and in the very waves off East Sands, while the next day 'Sabina' stated that she had heard haunting singing and smelt a distinctively sweet perfume on the deserted Castle Sands.

Online message boards are not exactly trustworthy monuments to probity and truth, so although the posts give a fascinating insight into the preoccupations of a number of students, it is hard to draw any firm conclusions about the veracity of the incidents. As an example of how false ghostly rumours can circulate, let us finish with the posts relating to University Hall, a residence on the North Haugh, with two sections being modern and the third, Wardlaw, dating from 1896. On 16 August 2003, 'diddy reese' passed on the usual rumours – there were rooms in Wardlaw closed off because of deaths by fire, or because a student had fallen to their death from a window – but then added an elaboration: apparently, one of the rooms was out of bounds because several years previously the student living there had become possessed, endured an exorcism, and was then moved to a mental institution. The following day 'Pussycat' responded, refuting the idea that any rooms in Wardlaw were blocked off, and noting that no-one, including the staff and long-term residents, had ever heard of the possession/exorcism episode. And a few weeks later, on 12 September, 'Precious' amusedly reported that there was a rumour in Wardlaw that two first year students had shared a specific bedroom in which they saw the furniture move by itself; as one of the named occupants of the 'haunted room', she was happy to point out that neither she nor her roommate had ever witnessed such a thing, and hence the 'haunting' was completely fabricated. It may be that a number of the other messageboard rumours, sightings and incidents had a similar genesis.

The Suicide Skeleton

> Preserved here likewise is the skeleton of an unfortunate man, formerly carrier to the university, who, about seventy or eighty years ago, put a period to his own existence.

This sentence in James Grierson's 1807 book *Delineations of St. Andrews,* introduces us to the curious case of the suicide, the skeleton, and the ghost that never was.

Norman Reid, Keeper of Manuscripts and Muniments, and Head of Special Collections at the University Library, summarised the episode in the University staff magazine *The Standard* (issue 13, March 2008). In January 1707, the University messenger, David Murray, committed suicide by hanging himself from the banister of the staircase in the King James library. As a form of post-mortem punishment for the sin of suicide, the University Court decreed that the man should 'hang for evermore'. His body was dissected, his skeleton articulated, and his bones laid in a specially-made coffin-like box which was then placed, feet down, on the very spot where he had ended his life. An inscription, in Latin, was attached to the box:

> You behold the remains of an unfortunate and infamous man, once the Messenger of this University of St Andrews and thereafter never to be named for all time to come: incensed at his monstrous action, in that he laid wicked hands upon himself and sought death by hanging, the sacred University, desiring to obtain the greatest advantage from one who had so criminally destroyed himself, resolved, first that his corpse should be publicly submitted to the dissecting knife, then that his bones should be articulated into

The Old Library on South Street. Suicide's skeleton not shown. (Photo by Geoff Holder)

1889, the ghoulish relic had been hidden away in a cupboard, away from the eyes of casual visitors. Finally, in 1941, George H. Bushnell, the University librarian, and Dr J.B. Salmond, a member of the University Court, located the box in the loft at the top of the staircase, and reopened it for the first time in many years. The bones were handed over to the Professor of Anatomy, for a study of the eighteenth-century method of articulation, and then, after 234 years, the unfortunate messenger's skeleton was given a proper burial. The box was burned.

The King James library is now part of the building known as the Old Library, a mix of eighteenth- and nineteenth-century architecture forming the block of St Mary's College that fronts onto South Street. George Bushnell, the librarian, incorporated the skeleton into the fictional ghost stories he wrote for the entertainment of the Students' Celtic Society during the blackouts of the Second World War. They were read aloud by candlelight, and were doubtless eerily effective. Bushnell published the stories as *A Handful of Ghosts* in 1945; in one, 'The Closing of the Cloisters', the messenger's skeleton becomes a murderous spirit seeking vengeance in the fog-bound cloisters of St Salvator's Quadrangle.

We noted above that rumours of ghosts were transmitted through the student population with often the slimmest relationship to objective reality. Yet, bizarrely enough, the presence of a complete honest-to-goodness skeleton – and that of a tragic suicide to boot – has not generated a single supernatural incident. Such is the curious, even fickle, nature of stories about ghosts.

a skeleton, on the 25 January in the year 1707 of the Christian Era; employing for that purpose the zealous services of one who at the time was Pharmacological-Surgeon and Botanist of the Dundee Society but now is a Doctor of Medicine of the Royal Society, Patrick Blair.

The skeleton was still on display 100 years later, when James Grierson noticed it. By

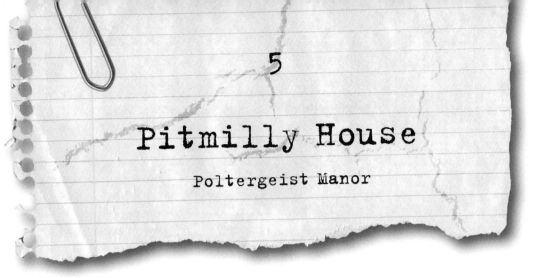

5

Pitmilly House

Poltergeist Manor

I do not know what the reader's reaction to the 'Poltergeist Manor' will be, but so far as I am concerned there is a *prima facie* case for serious – and scientific – investigation.

Harry Price, *Poltergeist over England*

SCOTTISH GHOST SETS MANSION
ON FIRE. INSURANCE PAID:
AN INSURANCE COMPANY
BELIEVES IN GHOSTS
MANSION FIRES MYSTERY

In April 1942, these, and similar headlines, could be found in newspapers from London to Adelaide. The press were intrigued because of the combination of a ghost and an insurance pay-out, but the details were scant. Twenty rooms within a Fife mansion had suffered damage by fire, while at other times heavy furniture had been heaped in the drawing room and jugs of water emptied over beds. The insurance company accepted that no human agency had been responsible for the incidents, and so paid up £400 for the damage. No dates were given and the location was not identified.

We now know that the fire broke out in March 1940; that the poltergeist activity commenced around 1936, and continued until the 1960s; and that the mansion where all this took place was Pitmilly House, near Kingsbarns, some eight miles south of St Andrews. Pitmilly (or Pitmillie – both spellings are used) no longer exists, to the point that it is impossible to locate even the site of the former house within the farmland that now covers it.

The poltergeist outbreak was one of the most amazing of such cases in British supernaturalism, yet there was no proper published report at the time, and many of the details remain obscure. In reconstructing this extraordinary story, I have relied on three principal sources: the book *Poltergeist over England*, written in 1945 by Harry Price,

Pitmilly House in the nineteenth century. (From A.H. Millar's Fife Pictorial and Historical, 1895)

the most famous psychical investigator of his era; *Pitmilly House: 'Poltergeist Manor'*, an excellently-detailed booklet published by St Andrews author Lorn Macintyre in 2011 ('Poltergeist Manor' was the coining of Harry Price); and the reminiscences of a witness, the late Jan Rostworowski, as passed to me by his daughter Basia Rostworowska and his nephew Paul Kieniewicz, both of whom I thank for their generosity. There is, no doubt, much more to uncover about the Pitmilly Poltergeist, but this is what we know so far.

The First Phase: 1936–1940

The construction of Pitmilly House commenced in the eighteenth century, but the principal front block was built in 1818, in a severe Georgian style. It was the residence of the Moneypennys – a prominent family who had owned the lands since 1211 AD. From the first years of the twentieth century, the mansion was let out to a variety of tenants, and in 1930 it was sold – the sale particulars detailing its four public rooms, nine bedrooms, four bathrooms, two dressing-rooms, six servants' bedrooms, and an extensive kitchen, all with electric lighting and central heating throughout. By the standards of the day, it was comfortable and well-appointed with modern facilities. The new owner was Captain John Arthur Jeffrey, the scion of an Edinburgh family, whose fortune derived from brewing. His wife, Alison, was regarded as the imperious ruler of her domain, a woman who refused to allow her daughter, Mary, to be educated outside the house, even though the highly-regarded St Leonard's girls' public school was just down the road in St Andrews. So while her brother, Ivan, went out into the wider world of 1930s society, Mary, trapped

at home, grew up unhappy and dissatisfied.

Although the connection is by no means universal, in many poltergeist cases the phenomena appear to cluster around one individual, the 'focus', typically a troubled child or young person. It is possible that Mary was the focus; the poltergeist seems to have commenced in 1936, when she was eleven years old. In that year, as the family sat down to dinner, a lump of coal appeared on the dining-room table as if out of nowhere. Such relocated objects are known as 'apports' and are absolutely typical of poltergeist cases: and they provide particular challenges to our view of the universe, as the removal and appearance of apports often seems to break the laws of physics.

In 1967, Ivan Jeffrey, who was born in 1915, gave an interview on the Radio 4 series *Scotland '67*. Combining what he told interviewer Tom Donald with the details from the 1945 book *Poltergeist over England*, we can piece together the extreme nature and scale of the poltergeist activities from 1936 to 1940. Many of the reports were supplied by an unnamed psychical investigator who visited the house in early 1940, at the height of the incidents. The phenomena included:

The transport of objects through the air. In early 1940, Ivan Jeffrey was assaulted by a Chinese bronze ornament flying down the hallway at him. Many other valuable items were seen to move through the air by multiple witnesses. Two people saw a fifteen-pound bronze jar zip through the open front door, turn through ninety degrees in mid-flight, and come to rest beside the garage. On another occasion, in the library, the psychical investigator narrowly avoided being hit by a flying ashtray. This same witness watched a bronze pot pushed off a high wardrobe, a tumbler smash into the corner of a room, and saw a large vase fly past him, thrown as if with great power. Objects were often thrown from the upper landing onto the half-landing below – items included a large Delft vase (it smashed, while its companion was relocated, unharmed, onto the stairs themselves) and a bulky, weighty chair.

The movement of furniture. Heavy items that would normally require two men to move, shifted about of their own volition. When so moving, they could not be restrained even by strong men. Two people watched a tall wardrobe tilt forward by forty-five degrees and hold itself suspended – thus defying the laws of gravity – before returning to its original stance. Three witnesses were struggling to move a self-moving chest of drawers back to its usual position when they saw a second chest of drawers some ten feet away topple over, smashing the china ornaments on it. Captain Jeffrey's bed jumped up and down. Large chests, which the psychical investigator could not even shift more than an inch, moved out from the walls and teetered at forty-five degrees.

Water damage. Any washing water kept in ewers in the bedrooms, was dumped onto the beds the moment the room was unoccupied.

Fire damage. Burning coals were often deposited in parts of the house, including rooms where there was no lit fire. Curtains, carpets and bedclothes were frequently scorched or burned; the investigator found burn marks in the most unlikely places, such as beneath a huge, heavy Victorian bed whose sides only allowed an inch of space of access to the floor, or on enamel tiles. On one occasion, a woman's hat was found on fire inside a wardrobe. A rolled-up blind some ten feet up the wall of the dining-room was burned through. In a bathroom, a towel was set on fire, while a shovel-full of coals appeared on the sofa in the library. To make things even weirder, Captain Jeffrey witnessed a small flame moving across the carpet in his bedroom. He attempted to beat it out with a pillow – *but the fire just dodged out of the way*. It did not seem to be actually burning the carpet, and so Captain Jeffrey put his hand over the flame – it was not hot. At this point the roving fire disappeared, leaving no scorch marks behind. Lady Ann Erskine, told Lorn Macintyre that on one occasion following a small fire, one of the Jeffrey women checked all the other rooms; every time she left a room, flames started up. Lady Erskine also recalled attending the sale of contents of the house after the Jeffreys died, and finding numerous small scorch marks on everything from bedspreads to carpets.

Attacks on pictures. On one occasion, while the drawing-room was unoccupied for less than five minutes, dozens of pictures in heavy frames were removed from the high and difficult-to-reach walls and dumped in the centre of the room. This action would have taken a man with a stepladder at least twenty minutes to accomplish. At another time, two paintings fell off the walls of the same room. Hearing the noise, several people came in and saw the fallen pictures, then returned to their business next door. When they re-entered the drawing-room a few minutes later, the paintings were back in place. Elsewhere, all the pictures in the library were found turned to the wall, and the psychical investigator found all the pictures on the upper stairs in a similar condition. He put them back – and fifteen minutes later found the same pictures lying on the stairs. A story related to Lorn Macintyre described how a female guest, descending the stairs, watched as the pictures lining the staircase rotated on their chains to face the wall.

Object relocation and movement. The same female guest mentioned above, placed her wet gloves to dry on the drawing-room fireplace – and when she returned the gloves were hovering in front of the fire, as if invisible hands were warming themselves. *Poltergeist over England* tells of a set of old and heavy fire-irons that were in such perpetual rattling motion that they were tied up with string; the knots then untied themselves and the irons continued their restlessness. On another occasion the irons turned up on the mantelpiece. The books of the library would be dumped on the floor. Mrs Jeffrey left her boudoir for a few moments, only to find that half a dozen pots of face cream and cosmetics had disappeared, along with a heavy Victorian mirror. The pots later reappeared in their original positions, but an immediate search revealed that the mirror had been relocated to a bedroom on the floor below. Another time, Mrs Jeffrey and the psychical investigator spent a quarter of an hour hunting out bronzes and vases that disappeared from the top floor, to be immediately found two flights below. A brace of pigeons in a game-bag vanished from the hall to the outside of the house. A bell rang of its own accord. A large bronze vase was found head down in the toilet. When two billiard balls starting playing up, Mrs Jeffrey hid them in the drive without telling anyone. A few days later the white ball was seen rumbling in the hall, and a check found that it had indeed been removed from its hiding place. A large hanging lamp on the half-landing was struck as if punched, and swung violently. A collection of used matches were taken from an ash-tray and arranged in regular two-inch intervals along the arm of the chair in which the investigator was sitting and smoking.

Attacks on individuals. Mary Jeffrey and her brother's wife, Vebeca, were preparing to go to bed when a pillow and bolster jumped up and hit Mary, while the bed lifted off the floor and shook with unrestrained violence. Her mother Alison rushed in to see the blankets and sheets floating off the bed onto the floor. As she leapt onto the bucking bed it seemed to calm down, but then a pillow was pulled out from beneath her and a chest of drawers glided into the centre of the room. Alison pushed the item back against the wall and leaned against it with the pillow as support, at which point the chest moved back to the middle again, shoving Alison helplessly along. The psychical investigator was pushed out of his chair and the chair deposited on top of him. Captain Jeffrey was attacked by another chair while coming down the stairs. Several members of the family were struck and injured by flying objects.

Attacks on religious visitors. The Jeffreys invited both Roman Catholic and Anglican clergymen to exorcize the poltergeist, to no effect – and during the prayers, books were thrown at the Catholic priest. According to one of Lorn Macintyre's correspondents – a cousin of the Jeffreys named Mrs Purvis of Earlshall – the Anglican priest was the Revd Piers Holt Wilson. Revd Wilson was the Dean of the Diocese of St. Andrews, Dunkeld and Dunblane (in 1943 he was became the Bishop of Moray, Ross and Caithness). On the day of the exorcism, Revd Wilson sat down in the big chair before the blazing fire in the drawing-room – only to have his hat whisked off his lap and into the fire, where it burned up.

The Great Fire. What may be termed the first phase of the haunting came to a climax during the daylight hours of Thursday, 7 March 1940, when seventeen separate fires broke out, damaging twenty rooms and causing an eighty-three-year-old woman servant to be rescued from her room by the fire brigade. After a slightly incredulous police investigation, this conflagration led to the insurance claim. In total more than £100 worth of damage was caused between 1936 and 1939, while the original insurance claim for the fire in March 1940 was £800 (the insurance company paid up only half).

On more than one occasion, the children and staff decamped to a cottage on the estate, returning home only when things seemed to calm down. Harry Price's informant, the anonymous psychical investigator, said he had signed statements from the principals in the house, and many other witnesses would be prepared to swear on oath as to what they had experienced. Sadly these statements have never come to public view.

The Second Phase: Pitmilly in the War Years

Captain Jeffrey died in 1941, aged fifty-one; his wife Alison followed him to the grave late the next year. From at least early 1941, Pitmilly was a station for Polish troops, although the Jeffreys continued to live there. In his radio interview from 1967, Ivan Jeffrey mentioned that some of the soldiers had reported unusual occurrences, such as 'bayonets stuck in walls', while *Poltergeist over England* has a brief mention of troops claiming to have seen a male ghost in the grounds – a claim which, to Harry Price, seemed rather dubious. Later in the war, the Women's Royal Naval Service (WRNS) took over Pitmilly, running it as a hospital for service personnel.

In 1942, the 'poltergeist insurance claim' story broke in the national press – for example, in both the *Daily Telegraph* and *Daily Mail* on 8 April – but the name of the mansion was kept secret, and so Pitmilly did not became a public spectacle. On 12 July of the same year, the sensationalist periodical *American Weekly* published an illustrated article on the case headlined: 'No Rest in the Mansion. Mean Plot of Incendiary spooks.' Once again Pitmilly was not mentioned, which was fortunate as the piece was less than scrupulously accurate, especially in the images – which conformed to the Hollywood stereotype of the Gothic haunted house. So, media-wise, Pitmilly remained undisturbed – which was something that could not be said to be the case within the house.

After the fall of France in 1940, many of the Polish forces fighting the Nazis regrouped in eastern Scotland, especially in the St Andrews area, where they guarded coastal defences. The mosaic on the side of the Town Hall on Queen's Gardens was created in October 1940, by three Polish soldiers – Wladzimierz Klocek, Jan Sterling and Swaryst Jakubowski – as a commemoration of the kindness shown to the Polish troops by the local people. One of these Polish soldiers, who arrived in 1940, was Jan Rostworowski, the twenty-one-year-old son of a noted playwright, Karol Hubert Rostworowski. Jan was a corporal in the First Rifle Brigade (Polish) and for some of the time his unit was based in and around Pitmilly, which was still occupied by the Jeffrey family at this time. In the

Jan Rostworowski, witness to the Pitmilly poltergeist. (Courtesy of Basia Rostworowska)

Jan's introduction to the activities of the poltergeist, and thereafter he witnessed an escalation of events. An ashtray flew through the air into the fireplace. Small fires broke out on the carpet in the very footsteps of Alison Jeffrey, Mary's mother – Jan and a servant beat the flames out with blankets. And most menacingly of all, a large wardrobe detached itself from the wall in the bedroom where Jan was reading, moved smoothly across the floor and rocked to and fro right next to Jan's bed, as if threatening him. Not unreasonably, the young man ran out and did not return to the house that night. The following morning it took the combined efforts of four soldiers to return the heavy wardrobe to its original position.

In a departure from the principal elements of the phenomena, Jan also claimed to have seen an apparition. According to his story, he was on sentry duty outside the house when he saw someone approaching. The figure did not respond to his challenge, and as it got nearer Jan realised that it was a woman wearing a long dress. She seemed very short, and, in the moonlight, it appeared her diminutive stature was due to the absence of her head.

Paul Kieniewicz admits that his uncle had a flair for the dramatic and a tendency to exaggerate during his vivid storytelling. So, while the poltergeist episodes ring true, I am not entirely convinced by the sighting of the headless ghost. Jan also claimed to have seen a document from an insurance company, politely declining coverage for fire damage on the house on the grounds that 'apparently the house was haunted'. Jan was something of a linguist and had been in Britain since May 1940, so it is possible that by 1941 his English was good enough to understand a complicated official document. However, once again I have some

nature of these things, especially in wartime, Jan wooed the seventeen-year-old Mary Jeffrey and the couple were quickly engaged, which meant the young Polish corporal was often staying at Pitmilly for reasons other than military duty.

The engagement did not last. From 1942 to 1945, Jan lived in London, working as a war correspondent. After the war, he went on to become a successful poet, but he did not write anything down about his adventures at Pitmilly. He died in 1975. He did, however, recount the experiences both to his daughter Basia and to his nephew Paul, and it is their memories that provide the next part of the story.

One day, Jan returned to his room to find his clothes and belongings disturbed and scattered. Thinking that Mary was for some reason upset with him, he confronted her, but of course she was innocent of the disturbance. This seems to have been doubts so I reserve judgment on the veracity on this episode.

We noted earlier that Mary Jeffrey was suggested as the focus for the poltergeist events, although this is, of course, not proven. In contrast, Jan appeared to believe that the psychic malevolence emanated not from Mary but from her father, Captain Jeffrey. Jan thought that the Captain's dislike of the foreigner engaged to his daughter erupted psychically in a display of unconscious aggression. As far as Jan was concerned, the poltergeist outbreaks were aimed at himself, with the intention of causing a split between the engaged couple. And, of course, the relationship did indeed founder. Mary Jeffrey served with the WRNS from 1943 to 1946, married in 1957, and died in 2000.

The Third Phase: Pitmilly after the War

When Harry Price published *Poltergeist over England* in 1945, he devoted a number of pages to the Pitmilly case, although once again he did not identify the house by name. It was his express intention to investigate Pitmilly. A few years earlier he had published *The Most Haunted House in England,* about a poltergeist in the infamous Borley Rectory in Essex. It is possible Price saw Pitmilly as a follow-up book entitled *The Most Haunted House in Scotland.* However he did not manage to visit Scotland before he died in 1948, and Pitmilly remained without any kind of proper investigation. One curiosity is that, within the hundreds upon hundreds of letters and personal notes within the archives of the Harry Price Library of Magical Literature at London University, there is not a single mention of Pitmilly. Price was an obsessive collator of his own correspondence, and in *Poltergeist over England* he quotes extensively from an anonymous source who had visited Pitmilly in 1940, apparently on more than one occasion. My contention is that this anonymous correspondent was J. W. Herries, the man who broke the insurance pay-out story in 1942. Herries was a stalwart of the Edinburgh Psychic College, as well as being the Chief Reporter for the *Scotsman.* But somehow these exchanges between Herries and Price have vanished.

After the war, the government returned the mansion to the Jeffrey family (Ivan and Mary). In June 1947, it was sold off as a hotel, the *East Fife Observer* noting that the house was famous for a ghost in the form of a Green Lady. This is the first time that a female apparition had been mentioned in print, so perhaps it is some kind of affirmation for Jan Rostworowski's claim to have seen a headless woman. The newspaper report, strangely enough, made no reference to the poltergeist incidents.

The mansion functioned as a hotel for almost two decades, although early dreams of it being a high-class resort for well-heeled foreign visitors did not entirely pan out, and by the 1960s the estate had gone downmarket as a site for holiday-makers spending their fortnights in static caravans. Before that happened, however, a wealthy newspaper owner from Wales stayed at Pitmilly House Hotel in the 1950s, using it as a base for golfing at St Andrews. According to an anecdote related to Lorn Macintyre, the millionaire moved out because of bizarre occurrences. His clothes draws were being emptied out onto the floor, and once he saw a line of fire running along the wall of a corridor for thirty yards. Once the flames had subsided, no scorchmarks could be found on the walls. This gentleman was almost certainly one of the Berry brothers, a pair of dynamic

Fleet Street entrepreneurs originally from Merthyr Tydfil. Between them William Berry and Gomer Berry, who died in 1954 and 1968 respectively, had variously owned *The Sunday Times, The Daily Telegraph, The Financial Times* and many other newspapers.

There were other episodes from this period. Lady Erskine told Lorn Macintyre that a lawyer friend was tasked with overseeing the alcohol at the hotel. One day he sealed the bottles of spirits and liqueurs as normal – but when he next checked them they were all empty, although the seals were intact. In August 1967, the Donaldsons, a prominent local family, visited Pitmilly and were told that in the previous few weeks a number of caravanners had left or had insisted on being moved to another site. What exactly had frightened them was unclear, but once again there were rumours of a Green Lady haunting the grounds.

The end, when it came, was ignominious. In March 1967, the owners of the hotel filed for bankruptcy. The house and grounds were sold to Mr J. Steven, a farmer, who absorbed everything into neighbouring Hillhead Farm. The mansion, which had a large crack down the front, languished in an abandoned state for a few months, but then it was partly destroyed by fire, and, on 4 December 1967, *The Courier* announced that 'THE MYSTERY HOUSE IS COMING DOWN'. The remaining stones were re-used to build houses in nearby Kingsbarns, and the site of Pitmilly mansion became entirely agricultural.

Although Pitmilly had never been the subject of a proper psychical investigation, its story did live on elsewhere, albeit in an altered (and pseudonymous) manner. In 1946, Frank Harvey wrote the play *The Poltergeist*, which went to have a successful West End run and then become popular on the regional circuit. Harvey had clearly been told the details by Price, with whom he had corresponded. He shifted the location from a Fife mansion to a rectory in Dartmoor, and centred the story on the Cockney assessor from the insurance company, who moves from suspecting fraud to becoming a believing victim of the poltergeist. A visiting psychical investigator manages to detach the spirit from its focus – the vicar's troubled daughter – but in so doing, transfers the poltergeist onto another female character, this time the maid. The pranks of the poltergeist form the basis of an ongoing series of physical comedy and sight gags. The farce was reworked in 1948, as the British low-budget film *Things Happen at Night,* written by St John Leigh Cloves and directed by Francis Searle at the film studios in Twickenham. The story is the same as that of the play, but to modern eyes the film appears creaky, slow and, production-wise, is unable to shake off its stilted origins on the stage. One curiosity is that the film starts with a fulsome set of thanks to – yes, you've guessed it – Harry Price.

Some Conclusions

What, in the end, can be said about this extraordinary episode? The sightings of the apparitions may or may not have been genuine, but, given the number and extent of witnesses, I consider there to be no doubt that the various physical phenomena – the moving and displacement of objects, the fires, the water damage, and the destruction – were objectively real. And we certainly have an insurance company – not the kind of culturally conservative organisation given to flights of fancy – agreeing with this conclusion. Pitmilly, by the way, may have been the first case where insurance was paid out for poltergeist damage, but it was not the last; in July 1952, several of the London papers reported that, after seven fires in nine months, and an investigation by a Scotland Yard forensics team, an insurance company paid out for a poltergeist claim on Pounsley Lodge, a large house in Sussex.

There is, of course, the possibility that, although the events were real, they were not supernatural in origin. We may suspect hoaxing by a servant or a member of the family, but while this may have happened on one or two occasions, the many events with multiple witnesses would seem to preclude this as an overall solution. In March 1964, G.W. Lambert wrote an article for the *Journal of the Society for Psychical Research* in which he attempted to match poltergeist reports with recordings of earth tremors. He noted that shocks were recorded on the nearby Ochil fault in 1936, 1937 and 1938, with even more activity in 1940. Although Pitmilly is not on the Ochil fault, Lambert showed that seismic events could be felt some distance from the geological faulting, especially if the watertable was high – the shock travelling through the water lines. As far as Lambert was concerned, the Pitmilly poltergeist was entirely explicable in terms of earthquakes and earth tremors. We do not have exact dates for the events at Pitmilly, so it is impossible to match them against seismological data. Even so, I have my doubts about this analysis. I suspect even a major earthquake would be unable to make a flying bronze jar turn ninety degrees in mid-flight, or create fires that did not burn, or remove pictures from a wall and stack them in a pile. Never mind arranging a group of matches in a regularly-spaced formation.

As to the notion that Mary Jeffrey was the unconscious psychic engine behind the incidents, that too falters if we accept that the phenomena lasted throughout the 1950s and '60s, long after Mary had quitted the mansion.

In the end, the 'Poltergeist Manor' remains an unanswered mystery. We know something spooky happened there – but we do not know how, or why.

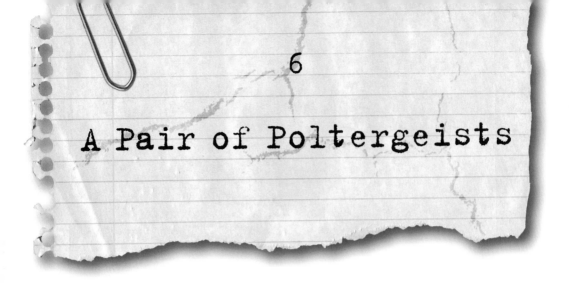

6

A Pair of Poltergeists

Be not afeard. The isle is full of noises.

William Shakespeare, *The Tempest*

IN September 1958, there was an apparent poltergeist incident in St Andrews. On the same day a long-running poltergeist outbreak reached its climax in Kirkcaldy, 23 miles away. Was this a coincidence? Or were the two events connected in some mysterious manner? Was the Kirkcaldy poltergeist even genuine?

On Saturday, 13 September 1958, the *Courier* had a story headlined:

NIGHT SCARE FOR THREE YOUNG MEN
Objects jump across bedroom
Is there a poltergeist in a St Andrews house?

The three musicians of 'Ian Dunn and his Trio' were coming to the end of their twelve-week residency at Rusack's Marine Hotel on Links Crescent. For generations, Rusack's had been *the* place to stay for serious golfers playing on the Links. The three young men – Ian Dunn (25), George Pitbladdo and Bob Macdonald (both 18) had been staying in a small two-storey annexe adjoining the hotel,

and, as usual, went to bed just after midnight. It was now the early hours of Friday the 12th September.

Within a few minutes of drifting off, all three musicians were woken by two thuds. When the light was switched on, they found a book that George Pitbladdo had been reading, and a salt cellar which was lying close to his bed, had both hit the wall close to Ian Dunn's bed. Puzzled but sleepy, they eventually turned off the light. Within a few seconds, there came another noise – and this time a thick leather belt belonging to Bob Macdonald had hit the wall in the same place, with so much force that the buckle had become detached from the leather. Two scarves had also flown through the air from one side of the room to another. The musicians kept the light on for the rest of the night, and reported the incidents to the under-manager at the hotel, who told the reporter: 'The three boys called me at 3 a.m. and they pointed out that the belt, the scarves, the salt cellar and the book had travelled from one side of the room to the other. They were certainly lying on the floor near Ian Dunn's bed.'

In 1959, G. W. Lambert mentioned the case in the *Journal of the Society for Psychical*

Research; Ian Dunn had told him that the phenomena continued for two more nights, that is, until the early hours of Sunday the 14th. A cup and dish, and an ink-bottle, were all thrown off the mantelpiece. The direction of the moving objects was always the same, from the 'free' end of the annexe towards the hotel. On the fourteenth the musicians vacated the annexe, as the summer season was over and their three-month residency had come to an end. No more incidents were reported from the premises.

Meanwhile, on the southeast coast of Fife, other strange things were happening within the same timescale. On the morning of Friday 12 September, Janet Forsyth rushed downstairs to tell her father that furniture had been moved about in the main bedroom. On investigating, James Forsyth found that the wardrobe had moved two feet from the wall, while a wicker chair had relocated from one side of the room to the window, which had been opened. This was the first time that the Forsyth household had witnessed the moving of furniture, although they had been plagued with apparently supernatural noises and minor physical phenomena for months.

James and Ida Forsyth had been living in the council house on Oaktree Square, Kirkcaldy, since early 1957. They had nine children, aged between fifteen years and nine months. The house had been built in 1947. In February 1958, the family started to hear footsteps on the upstairs landing. Then closed drawers started to jump open with no obvious cause. Mr Forsyth tried sticking cardboard under the drawers, but the next day they were open once again. The family dog refused to go upstairs at the times when the 'spirit' was apparently active. The noises got worse, and the health

Rusacks Hotel from the Links. (Photo by Geoff Holder)

of the children started to suffer. Mr Forsyth, a thirty-seven-year-old coal merchant, found himself unable to work because he was awake all night trying to deal with the ghost.

Eventually the story reached the press. On Tuesday, 9 September 1958, the *Courier* printed a piece with the headline: COUNCIL HOUSE 'GHOST' TERRIFIES FIFE FAMILY. It was reported that on the previous Sunday the Forsyths had invited Archibald McIlhatton, of neighbouring Veronica Crescent, to spend the night in the house. It seemed to be an attempt at validation: Mr McIlhatton was a self-described 'doubting Thomas' and a stranger to the Forsyths. The family clearly wanted an independent opinion.

The thirty-nine-year-old told the *Courier* reporter what happened:

> During the night I heard six bumps like the sound of a walking stick and then there were the noises of a scuffle on the stairs as if a fight was going on between two men. I heard drawers opening after that and the sound of them being dragged along the floor. I found doors and drawers open and the cardboard I had used to jam them lying on the floor.

As agreed with the family, Mr McIlhatton left at 3 a.m., taking four of the Forsyth children home with him. He noted that one of the children, a fourteen-year-old girl, was 'stiff with fright' and had started stammering. She refused to go back home, while Mrs Forsyth starting sleeping over at a friend's house, and had to be prescribed sedatives by a doctor. 'We must have some rest from this thing,' she said, 'it's been going on for seven months, getting worse all the time.' On the Monday, all nine of the children, having been refused accommodation at St Olaf's Children's Home for the night, were sleeping at friends' and neighbours', leaving James Forsyth alone in the house. He wanted to be rehoused and decided to refuse to pay his rent until a council official, or a member of the Town Council, spent a night in the haunted house.

The story became a fixture in the local press for the next four weeks, with stories in the *Courier* on 10, 11, 13, 15, 20, 23 and 26 September, and on 2 and 8 October. On the night of Monday 8th, James Forsyth undertook an all-night vigil in the house, accompanied by some of his neighbours, along with John Lees, the Kirkcaldy council housing factor, and Councillor James Barron. Also present on the Monday night was a psychic investigator, Mrs Margaret Neil of Edinburgh, who claimed that she saw an apparition in the living room about 3 a.m. This figure resembled a nine-year-old boy, standing with an older person in the corner. The Forsyths had a boy who died in infancy. He would now have been aged nine. Mr Forsyth had previously seen a spiritualist about the haunting, and had been told that the incidents were caused by the spirit of a suicide trapped in the house. A suggestion had been raised in the press that the house had been used for séances by a previous occupant, but this was denied by the tenant, Mrs May Smith, who had lived in the house for a decade. Her mother, Mrs Mary Kidd, was a spiritualist, but during the six months she had stayed at Oaktree Square, no séances or other spiritualistic activity had taken place. 'If there is an entity in the Forsyths' home,' said Mrs Kidd, 'it must have come with them. I suspect it is someone who has passed on, and the spirit, being earth-bound, wants to join them.'

A *Courier* reporter spent most of the Monday night in the house, and heard nothing unusual, although he did state that:

> Mr and Mrs Forsyth are utterly convinced there are forces at work in the house. They report windows opening, hearing footsteps in empty rooms, and drawers being opened. Their distress is real, and Mrs Forsyth appears to be on the verge of a breakdown.

Early on the Tuesday morning, James Forsyth collapsed with exhaustion. Neither the housing factor nor the councillor, however, experienced anything bizarre in the Oaktree Square dwelling, and remained unconvinced about the request for rehousing. However, much to James Forsyth's relief, Marcel Jankowsky, then occupying a council house on Laurel Crescent, offered to do a straight swap with the distressed family. Mr Jankowsky said he did not believe that the house was haunted, but just in case, he wanted a clause inserted in the agreement stating that, 'if strange bumps and sounds are heard he will be offered another house'.

The publicity brought out the usual suspects. On Tuesday night, a crowd of forty teenagers turned up, many of whom waited most of the night in the street for something paranormal to take place, disturbing the neighbours with their noise. On Wednesday evening, an evangelist from Kinghorn called in, spending half an hour with the family and blessing the house. Two mediums arrived about midnight. Correspondence from psychics and Christians started arriving by the sackload. Meanwhile, five of the Forsyth children were sleeping in several addresses scattered across Kirkcaldy. Then on the Friday morning (12 September) came the report of the movement of the furniture, a definite escalation of what had gone before. To confuse matters, however, the evangelist, Mrs Hope Mullin, said that she and her husband had been responsible for moving the wardrobe and chair and opening the window. This had been on Wednesday night, but the Forsyths discovered the rearranged furniture on Friday morning. Then the council revealed that the close (or open passage) that ran between the Forsyths' home and the neighbouring property, had just been repaired because the ceiling was cracked. The close passed under one of the bedrooms. 'The ceiling was repaired because it was thought to be dangerous,' said a council official. 'It may have been pressure from the adjoining walls that caused the damage, but there were marks on the ceiling which may have been caused by a rake or a broomhead.' The short close was open from both

ends and easily accessible. So perhaps the noises and movements were caused by a malicious individual banging on the ceiling with an implement – although to keep that up, undetected, for seven months, was a truly heroic degree of nuisance-making.

Mr Forsyth, however, was having none of this, and firmly believed in the ghost. 'We'll never be free of this thing so long as we live in this house,' he said. On the Wednesday, after another sleepless night, James Forsyth visited Marcel Jankowsky's council house on Laurel Crescent, but turned down the swop because the lobby was too dark and he feared his wife and children would be too frightened to sleep in the house. Mr Forsyth wrote to both the council and his MP requesting another house.

On Thursday 18 September, Tom Hubbard, MP for Kirkcaldy, spent the night in the 'haunted house'. His verdict: 'To say there is a ghost there is sheer nonsense.' Mr Hubbard did not hold back in his opinions:

> I went to the house prepared to believe Mr Forsyth and his wife genuinely thought there was something there. Instead Mr Forsyth said I would hear nothing, but that he could set up conditions at any time which would allow the ghost to be heard.

This sounds damningly like accusations of a hoax. 'After spending five hours in the house,' continued the MP, 'I'm convinced he has conjured the whole thing up in his mind. The tragedy of the whole affair is the effect it has had on the children's minds.'

Things did not get any better for the Forsyths. On Tuesday 23 September, it was revealed that the education authorities in Kirkcaldy had threatened them with prosecution unless their six children of school age attended classes. It seemed that six of the children had not been in school for the previous fortnight. 'The children are so terrified they can't sleep at night and have to get tablets,' said Mr Forsyth. 'When they waken in the morning they are not fit to go to school. They are all really keen on school, but can't go when they have not had enough sleep.' As a result of the letter, however, the six children had returned to school – but in the afternoons only. Then on Friday 26 September, the family were told they would be evicted if they did not pay their rent arrears. James Forsyth, who had been off work with the stress of the haunting, was adamant that he would repay the debt of £16 as soon as the council re-housed his family, but he was clearly on a losing wicket. On Thursday 2 October, it was reported that, having paid off his arrears with the help of a loan from friends, Mr Forsyth and his family had succeeded in getting a new house, this one on Wright Place. However, he had fallen behind with payments for his delivery van, and was threatened with it being repossessed – and hence he would be unable to carry on his business as a sea-coal merchant. Even now, on the eve of the move, the ghostly noises had not stopped – the linoleum in the upstairs bedrooms had been lifted, and as a result phantom footsteps were being heard, as if of a person walking on bare wooden boards.

What, if anything, can be concluded from the story of the 'Kirkcaldy poltergeist'? At least one of the neighbours witnessed strange noises and sights, so it would seem that at least some of the incidents were objectively real, that is, they were not simply imaginative products of the family's collective anxieties. It has already been noted that more than one observer at the time suggested that the whole thing was a hoax. There was the possibility that all, or some, of the noises had been created by someone

banging on the ceiling of the open passage of the close – the ceiling that formed the floor of one of the bedrooms. Perhaps the Forsyths had a neighbour who resented the noise made by the nine children, and banged on the passage ceiling late at night out of malice, or conceivably one of the three teenagers in the family was sneaking out of the house and hitting the surface of the close with a broom. Tom Hubbard MP clearly suspected the family were behind the noises, while the sole occasion of macro-phenomena – the relocation of the wardrobe and chair – may well have been simply the result of the visiting evangelists moving furniture about. On 8 October 1958, the *Courier* reported that Mr and Mrs Alex Dewar, the new tenants of the Oaktree Square house, were convinced that all the noises were just caused by the faulty plumbing. Labelling the entire episode 'an absolute farce,' Mrs Dewar said:

The cistern in the bathroom needs repairs, and it sometimes makes weird noises. There's also a dripping tap in the bathroom which echoes round the house when everything else is quiet.

Could there have been genuine phenomena? Certainly the Forsyths thought so, although this on its own proves nothing. The incidents were not investigated by any kind of competent psychical investigators, and so all we have to go on are the newspaper reports, which of course may have omitted key information, simply because it did not seem newsworthy. It seems highly unlikely that the Forsyths had any kind of ghost-manufacturing plan to persuade the council to rehouse them – for a start, they appeared happy with the original house, and, more tellingly, they suffered psychologically, emotionally and financially.

We have little information on the situation within the family, although we can suspect that with nine children under one roof, there may well have been internal tensions. The four oldest children were all girls, and so fit into the stereotype of the 'troubled female adolescent' often associated with poltergeist outbreaks. To counter this, however, there is nothing in the newspaper accounts that links any of the children directly to the phenomena, and there is no hint of any kind of 'focus'.

In 'Scottish Haunts and Poltergeists: A Regional Study', the article published in the 1959 *Journal of the Society for Psychical Research,* and mentioned above in connection with the Rusack's Hotel incidents, G.W. Lambert came up with an altogether different interpretation. His suggestion was that the St Andrews and Kirkcaldy incidents were indeed real, but were not supernatural in origin. Lambert consulted *Whitaker's Almanac* and found that 'high water' warnings had been issued for the Fife coast for both for the periods 5-9 February and 14-17 September 1958 – remember, the Kirkcaldy noises started in February. His view was that high tides set up seismic resonances in the coastal rock formations, and that these pressures could cause localised tremors that would not show up on conventional seismographs. Rusack's Hotel annexe in St Andrews and Oaktree Square in Kirkcaldy, both experienced 'poltergeist' activity from 12-14 September because they were both on the coast, and both affected by local earth movements resulting from strong high tides.

As an explanatory notion, this is an attractive idea. It suggests a geophysical mechanism that explains why two apparent poltergeist incidents took place on the same date but more than twenty miles apart. It seems to offer a sop to both those who believe the phenomena were real, and those who are sceptical about the supernormal causes of the phenomena. However, I remain unconvinced, largely because the data is so poor. We are told that the Kirkcaldy incidents lasted intermittently for seven months, but we do not have any specific dates until September, so it is impossible to match the phenomena to high tides or other geophysical events. Lambert focused on the macro-event of the relocated furniture at Oaktree Square, but as we have seen there may be a quite mundane cause for this – in which case, the postulated link with the St Andrews incidents is false. Also, Lambert's dates do not quite match up – the high water warning was for 14-17 September, while the Rusack's incidents commenced on the 12th. With the best will in the world, it is hard to forge a convincing link between the records of tides and the disparate phenomena over an extended period, especially in the Kirkcaldy case. Of course, there may indeed have been something going on under the foundations of Oaktree Square and the Rusack's annexe – but we have no way of knowing this, although in the case of the three musicians, the simplest solution may indeed be some kind of earth tremor, especially since the direction of the moving objects was consistent. In the end, however, Lambert's analysis remains an intriguing idea, but poor on evidence.

As for the long-term 'haunting' at Oaktree Square, I suspect that – whether caused by malign human agency, faulty plumbing or subterranean rumblings – the noises were indeed real. What seems to have happened is that the mysterious sounds were interpreted as supernatural in origin, with the result that a kind of domestic hysteria raged through the household, reaching a climax with the unfortunate events in September 1958. The Forsyths had no further visitations in their new council house, and their successors as tenants in the original house experienced nothing untoward. I therefore suggest that the Kirkcaldy ghost panic probably did *not* have a paranormal dimension.

On 25 October 2000, 'Sophie' from St Andrews wrote to Katie Coutts, the resident psychic on *The Sun* tabloid, with a description of a poltergeist manifestation. After living in the house undisturbed for eight years, it was decided to renovate the attic as a bedroom for the youngest daughter, who appears to have been in her teenage years. It was at this point that things started to happen. The television in the girl's bedroom turned itself on and off. The volume increased or decreased without reason. The iron switched on. Items were relocated around the attic. Footsteps were heard from the empty room. The psychic suggested the phenomena were focused on a large doll propped up in the corner of the attic, and recommended throwing it out immediately. Poltergeists are still with us, it seems.

7

Death Warnings, Dead Air and Ghost Villages

Once one crosses the border into Scotland, one finds oneself not only in a land of penetrating beauty, but in the land of Faëry, the very atmosphere of which seems impregnated with the spirit of long-gone Ages. Every house has its ancestral hauntings; every village its traditional Spooks; every housewife and her man their individual tales of uncanny happenings.

A.M.W Stirling, *Ghosts Vivisected*, 1958

Omens of death

One of the most common themes running through Scottish ghost lore and folklore, is the idea of the death wraith, an apparition of living person. If the wraith is seen, it presages the imminent death of that person. In variants on this theme, a person may have a longstanding presentiment that their death will be signalled by a particular sign, while many noble families passed down an internal tradition that the appearance of a certain animal or supernatural figure was an omen of immediate death. In the St Andrews area, we have examples of all three.

In 1932, H.J. Rose wrote to the journal *Folklore* with an intriguing example of the death-warning. A jobbing gardener working away in the greenhouse of a St Andrews house, was surprised to see his elderly employer tapping at the glass to attract his attention, as the old man was in poor health, with limited mobility. Leaving the greenhouse, the gardener found only the old man's daughter in the garden, but she not been tapping and had not seen her father anywhere. Within the house, the gardener found the old man asleep in a chair, and it was clear he had not ventured outside for several hours. The gardener then told several people that the elderly gentleman would be dead in four days; and this turned out to be the case. The truly unusual aspect of the case is the precise predicted date, and I can think of no parallel in the literature for a death prediction of exactly four days.

In 1879, George Gourlay of Anstruther published *Fisher Life; or, The Memorials of Cellardyke and the Fife Coast*, which contained the tale of a fisherman named Alexander Dick. The young man had long held a presentiment that, like his brother before him, he would die at sea. 'I know I will be drowned one day,' he would tell his friends. When asked why he still continued to fish, he replied, 'I am not afraid; God numbers our days, and Heaven is as near to us at sea as it ever is or can be on land.' On 30 July 1856, Alexander Dick was thrown from his herring boat, and sank so quickly that his companion barely caught a glimpse of the upturned face sinking beneath the waves.

Sir Archibald William Montgomerie, the 13th Earl of Eglinton, was a nineteenth-century Tory politician and an aficionado of the sporting world – once taking his love of horse riding to the extreme of promoting a medieval-type jousting tournament. He died on 4 October 1861. In 1879 William Henderson's *Folk-Lore of the Northern Counties of England and The Borders* revealed the legend of his death. The Earl was playing golf on the links of St Andrews when he suddenly stopped in the middle of a game, saying, 'I can play no longer, there is the Bodach Glas. I have seen it for the third time; something fearful is going to befall me.' That night, as he was handing a candlestick to a lady who was retiring to her room, he expired. Henderson received the story from a clergyman who was witness to the events.

The *Bodach Glas,* Gaelic for the 'Gray Man' or 'Gray Messenger', is a standard feature of Celtic supernatural folklore – the tall figure dressed in a gray plaid being a frequently cited death-omen among prominent families. Sir Walter Scott used it in the *Waverley* novels. William Henderson only gave the name of the nobleman as 'The Earl of E', but he is named as Lord Eglinton in *Real Ghost Stories*, published in 1921, by William T. Stead.

Not all apparitions are fatal. In 1903, Dr F.A. Rorie wrote a series of articles on local ghost stories for the *Fifeshire Advertiser.* He described the case of a woman who saw her own wraith passing by the window when she was making the bed. She knew that it meant either imminent death or long life. In her case it was the latter, as she lived to be ninety-two.

'Crisis apparitions' are the appearance of someone's spirit at a distance, while they are dying or lying ill elsewhere. Once again, there are many examples in the literature of ghosts. Catherine Crowe's classic study of the supernatural, *The Night-Side of Nature,* published in 1848, features a case linked to St Andrews. Mrs K., the wife of the provost of Aberdeen, clearly saw her brother through the front window of her home, and hurried out to meet him. When he was not at the front door, she went round to the back; but her brother was nowhere to be seen. Shortly afterwards, news arrived from St Andrews that her brother had died in his home there; and, as far as could be made out, he expired at the same time his apparition was seen in Aberdeen.

A Vortex of Evil

Something unique in the supernatural history of St Andrews took place in June 1906. Mary Butts, a sixteen-year-old pupil at St Leonard's School, was walking fast along the bays and headlands south of the town. It was the final week of term, and the unhappy, introspective student was looking forward to leaving the school for the last time. She was relishing the solitude and the mid-morning play of wind and sunlight, when, half-way across a cove, she stepped into what she described as 'a *focus,* a column of energy, cold and vile and hateful... dead, spinning cold.' It seemed to her that a patch of air on the beach was 'dead': 'An air-pool, it was grey and whirling and as if full of specks.' She was temporarily blinded by the experience, and had to wrench herself

The Spindle Rock on the St Andrews coast. Somewhere near here Mary Butts encountered a 'vortex of evil.' (From Fifeshire *by E.S. Valentine, 1910)*

out of the 'evil' spot, whereupon she was compelled to sink onto a rock to recover her strength and senses. The sun was still shining, and the spot on the beach bore no outward marks of disturbed air – but on her return journey home she deliberately took the longer cliff-path, rather than the short-cut via the beach. Butts told no-one at the time and the episode only appeared in 1937, in her autobiography *The Crystal Cabinet*. The passage is replete with words such as 'terror', 'fear', 'inimical' and 'deadly' – she was clearly profoundly affected by the experience. Butts did not identify the cove where the incident took place, and could find no tradition of dark deeds or events associated with the beach.

Mary Butts was an unusual character. She was sent to St Andrews from her beloved home in Dorset, and was desperately unhappy at St Leonard's. After the First World War, she plunged into the *demi-monde* of Bohemian Europe, writing modernist fiction, experimenting with sexuality, relationships and drugs, meeting artists such as Jean Cocteau (who illustrated one of her works), and visiting the occultist Aleister Crowley at his infamous 'Abbey of Thelema' in Sicily. She died in 1937. Although she had a small number of visionary experiences later in life, Butts never again encountered anything that engendered the sense of blinding terror she felt in that mysterious pool of 'dead air' on a Fife beach.

The Phantom Hamlet of Dunino

An even more extraordinary event was recorded by James Wilkie in *Bygone Fife from Culross to St Andrews*. At a time in the late nineteenth or early twentieth century, when travel by horse was still commonplace, a visitor, riding from the south coast of Fife to St Andrews, decided to make a detour to visit the church at Dunino. From the flank of a hill, just north-east of the church, the traveller paused to admire the view, in particular the picturesque hamlet on the north side of the Dunino Burn:

> Some of the cottages were thatched, some tiled; but all were covered with roses and creepers. In front a strip of garden, stretching to the burn, was trimly kept, and full of old-world flowers; behind, it took on more the nature of a kail-yard. At the east end, on slightly higher ground, a smithy closed the prospect.

The rider was enchanted with the scene, which seemed to him to be a veritable idyll:

> No sound broke the stillness of the summer noon but the flow of the burn. At one or two of the doors there stood an old man in knee-breeches and broad bonnet, or a woman in a white mutch and a stuff gown, while in the entrance to the forge the smith leant motionless on his hammer.

Sighing contentedly, the traveller moved on to inspect Dunino Church, and then rode the remaining four and a half miles to St Andrews. In the autumn of the following year, he returned this way with a companion, to whom he wished to show 'the most old-world hamlet in Fife'. The pair stopped at the exact same location, preparing to drink in the view.

There was no hamlet to be seen; no cottages, no garden, no roses or creepers, no smithy – just a small, decrepit-looking croft that looked as if it had stood on the spot for many years. Wilkie told his readers that he had been informed 'on excellent authority' that at least three or four cottages, plus a blacksmith's shop, had once stood on the spot; as far as he was concerned, the traveller had been vouchsafed a glimpse of a hamlet that had ceased to exist many years previously. It was an example of a 'time-slip', where people in the present experience a temporary vision of an earlier time. Analysing the description of the vision, it seems to indicate a scene from the 1700s. White mutches were linen caps kept tied under the chin; by the end of the eighteenth century they were moving out of fashion, and were being mostly worn by older women. Stuff gowns were from the same period, being heavy coarse woollen dresses worn in autumn and winter. The knee-breeches and bonnets suggested working men of the 1700s or the early 1800s. If this was indeed a time-slip, then the Dunino case was a classic of its kind. But when author Helen Cook investigated the incident for *The Scots Magazine* in 1985, she discovered the story was even stranger than had been supposed.

Cook followed the directions given in Wilkie's account, taking the public footpath from the St Andrews/Anstruther road and crossing the bridge across the burn. From here a short diversion into the flank of the hill provided a view looking north over Dunino Burn, to the spot where the unnamed rider saw the visionary cottages. With this as her guide, she then turned to old maps and documents in an effort to establish the reality of any previous hamlet on the spot.

None of the standard reference works – such as *The Statistical Account of Scotland* (1791-99), *The New Statistical Account of Scotland* (1845) and *A Descriptive & historic gazetteer of the counties of Fife, Kinross & Clackmannan* (1857) mention any hamlet for the given location, although their descriptions about buildings are not always precise. General William Roy's 1755 map of Fife shows buildings on both sides of the burn, but the map is usually thought to be inaccurate when showing micro-locations. The 1775 map from *The Counties of Fife and Kinross* does show three buildings marked 'Hillside' just north of the burn, and two more buildings at 'Violet' a short distance away. These structures, now long vanished, would have been visible to the visitor, although they do not match exactly his description of the hamlet, and when the same buildings are shown in a later map of 1827, they are in different locations to those shown on the maps of 1755 and 1775. As for blacksmiths, there was one in the general area in the nineteenth century, but neither of the two consecutive locations given for the smithy – at 'Tosh' in 1864 and 'Pathhead' in 1889 – were in any way visible from the viewpoint taken by the traveller.

The documentary evidence, then, is inconclusive, especially as the early maps are contradictory. There is no evidence for a smithy on the site of the vision, and no direct evidence for a hamlet in the exact area – although we cannot be certain there was *not* a row of cottages there at some point. Wilkie does not give us the name of the witness, nor the date the vision occurred, and there are no other verifiable details. In the end, it is impossible to tell whether what was experienced was objectively 'real', or entirely subjective and internal. Was it a genuine time-slip of a hamlet that had once existed on the spot? Or an impression of a place from elsewhere in Scotland? Or even a vision of somewhere that had never existed? There is a minor branch of the literature of the supernatural that deals with 'perfect places' – people find themselves in the perfect pub, hotel, or country village, and, after leaving, discover that the place never actually existed. It is clear from the original account that the witness regarded the peace and tranquillity of the old-world hamlet as a 'perfect place'. There is another clue in the account – the people in their old-fashioned costumes seemed to be stationary, idealised motionless figures in a sunlit paradise. This suggests the visitor may have been in a light trance or altered state, and the account describes how he tore himself away from the sight 'half in a dream'.

Dunino itself is a location with an uncanny heritage. The church and churchyard incorporate the remnants of a Bronze Age stone circle that once stood on the site. To the west of the parish church, a flight of stone steps leads down to the dell of Dunino Den, in which can be found two potholes linked to legends of Celtic saints, Culdee monks and encounters with the Devil. The potholes, on Altar Rock and Pulpit Rock, may be natural or could have been hollowed out by hand. Also in the Den is the carving of a footprint – which, if ancient, suggests a link with early ideas of king making ceremonies. Nearby carvings of a wheel-headed Celtic cross and a piece of Celtic knot work are relatively modern, and the dell is decorated with a range of pagan offerings and symbols; for some people Dunino Den is clearly a sacred site. Is any of this suggestive that Dunino is a place that engenders visionary experiences? In 2009, I was contacted by a local resident who briefly mentioned experiencing something weird and ghostly on 17 February 1998. To my great regret, I was tardy in following up the report, and the individual passed away before we could communicate further. Is it just a coincidence that the only detail mentioned in the email was that the experience took place between the back of the church and the road – close to the very spot where the unnamed traveller had his original vision of the mysterious hamlet…?

Miracles have never really ceased, but continue daily in our midst, often unknown, unheeded, and unsolved. We have still very much to learn.
W.T. LInskill, *The Haunted Tower*, 1925

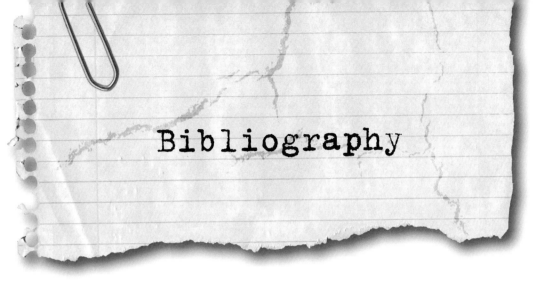

Bibliography

Books and Pamphlets

Bower, Walter, *Scotichronicon* Book VI, D.E.R. Watt (ed.), Aberdeen University Press/Mercat Press; Aberdeen & Edinburgh, 1995

Bushnell, George H., *A Handful of Ghosts*, St Andrews Preservation Trust; St Andrews, 1993 (first published 1945)

Butts, Mary, *The Crystal Cabinet: My Childhood at Salterns*, Beacon Press; Boston, Massachusetts, 1988 (first published 1937)

Cant, Ronald Gordon, *The University of St Andrews – A Short History*, St Andrews University Library; St Andrews, 1992

Cook, Helen, *A Haunting of Ghosts and an Unsolved Mystery of St Andrews*, David Winter & Son; Dundee, 1983

Council of St Leonard's School, *Queen Mary's House and those who lived in it*, Council of St Leonard's School; St Andrews, 1977

Cowan, Ian B., *The Scottish Reformation*, Weidenfeld and Nicholson; London, 1982

Crawford, Robert (ed.), *The Book of St Andrews*, Polygon; Edinburgh, 2007

Crowe, Catherine, *The Night-Side of Nature, or, Ghosts and Ghost-Seers*, T. C. Newby; London, 1848

Fawcett, Richard, *St Andrews Cathedral*, Historic Scotland; Edinburgh, 1999

Fleming, David Hay, *Hand-Book to St Andrews and Neighbourhood*, J. & G. Innes, St Andrews Citizen Office; St Andrews, 1897

———— *Howkings in St Andrews Cathedral and its Precincts in 1904* (reprinted from the *St Andrews Citizen*; 1905?)

Geddie, John, *The Fringes of Fife*, W. & R. Chambers; Edinburgh & London, new edition 1927

Gordon, J.F.S., *Monasticon*, John Tweed; Glasgow, 1868

Gordon, Margaret Maria, *The Home Life of Sir David Brewster*, David Douglas; Edinburgh, 1881

Gourlay, George, *Fisher Life; or, The Memorials of Cellardyke and the Fife Coast*, Fife Herald Office; Cupar, 1879

Green, Andrew, *Our Haunted Kingdom*, Fontana; London, 1975

———— *Ghosts of Today*, Kaye & Ward; London, 1980

Grierson, James, *Delineations of St. Andrews,* Peter Hill, St Andrews; and Vernor, Hood & Sharpe, London; 1807

Hamilton, David, 'The Haunted Major Revisited' in *Through the Green* Issue 83, December 2007

Henderson, William, *Folk-Lore of the Northern Counties of England and The Borders,* The Folk-Lore Society, W. Satchell, Peyton & Co.; London, 1879

Henry, David, *Sketches of Medieval St Andrews,* St Andrews; 1912

Herkless, John, and Hannay, Robert Kerr, *The College of St. Leonard,* William Blackwood & Sons; Edinburgh & London, 1905

Kirk, Russell, *St Andrews,* BT Batsford; London, 1954

Lamont-Brown, Raymond, *Phantoms of the Theatre,* Satellite Books; London, 1978

———— *The Life and Times of St Andrews,* John Donald; Edinburgh, 1989

Lang, Andrew, *St Andrews,* Longmans, Green & Co.; London, 1893

Linskill, W.T., *St Andrews Ghost Stories,* J. & G. Innes, St Andrews Citizen Office; St Andrews, 1911

———— *The Strange Story of St Andrews Haunted Tower,* St Andrews Citizen; St Andrews, n.d.

Macfarlane, Walter, *Genealogical Collections Concerning Families in Scotland, Made by Walter Macfarlane 1750-1751* James Toshach Clark (ed.), Scottish History Society; Edinburgh, 1900

McRoberts, David (ed.), *The Medieval Church of St Andrews,* John S. Burns & Sons; Glasgow, 1976

Marshall, Robert, *The Haunted Major,* Scottish Academic Press; Edinburgh & London, 1983 (first published 1902)

Marshall, Rosalind K., *John Knox,* Birlinn, Edinburgh, 2000

Morton, H.V., *In Search of Scotland,* Methuen & Co.; London, 1968 (first published 1929)

Paterson, Alexander Brown, *The Tale o' the Toon: St. Andrews through the eyes of A.B. Paterson, Vol. 1, to 1945,* A. B. Paterson; St Andrews, 1982

Price, Harry, *Poltergeist: Tales of the Supernatural,* Senate; London, 1994 (first published in 1945 as *Poltergeist over England*)

Reid, Norman, 'The skeleton of St Mary's' in *The Standard* No. 13, March 2008

Robertson, James K., *About St Andrews – And About,* Citizen Office; St Andrews, 1973

Rogers, Charles, *History of St Andrews with a full account of the Recent Improvements in the City,* Adam & Charles Black; Edinburgh, 1849

Salmond, J.B. (ed.), *Andrew Lang and St Andrews,* University of St Andrews; St Andrews, 1948

Sanderson, Margaret H.B., *Cardinal of Scotland: David Beaton c.1494-1546* John Donald; Edinburgh, 1986

Schulenburg, Jane Tibbetts, *Forgetful of their sex: female sanctity and society, ca. 500-1100,* University of Chicago Press; Chicago, 1998

Simpkins, John Ewart, *County Folk-Lore Vol. VII. Examples of Printed Folk-Lore Concerning Fife with some Notes on Clackmannan and Kinross-Shires,* The Folklore Society/Sidgwick & Jackson; London, 1914

Stead, William T. (ed. Estelle W. Stead), *Real Ghost Stories,* George H. Doran Co.; New York, 1921

Taylor, James W., *Historical Antiquities of Fife,* Hunter & Co.; Edinburgh, 1875

Tobert, Michael, *Pilgrims in the Rough: St Andrews beyond the 19th Hole,* Luath Press; Edinburgh, 2000

Underwood, Peter, *Gazetteer of Scottish Ghosts,* Fontana/Collins; Glasgow, 1975

Wilkie, James, *The History of Fife from the Earliest Times to the Nineteenth Century,* William Blackwood & Sons; Edinburgh and London, 1924

———— *Bygone Fife from Culross to St Andrews*, William Blackwood & Sons; Edinburgh and London, 1931

Wodrow, Robert, *Analecta, Or, Materials for a History of Remarkable Providences; Mostly Relating to Scottish Ministers and Christians* 4 Vols., Maitland Club; Edinburgh, 1842-1843

Wodrow, Robert (ed. James Maidment), *Private Letters, Now First Printed from the Original Mss., 1694-1732*, W. Aitkin; Edinburgh, 1829

Young, Douglas, *St Andrews: Town & Gown, Royal & Ancient*, Cassell; London, 1969

Journals and Magazines

Cook, Helen, 'The Unsolved Mystery of St Andrews' in *Scotland's Magazine*, August 1975

———— 'Haunted St Andrews' in *The Scots Magazine* Vol. 110, No.2, November 1978

———— 'The Dunino Vision' in *The Scots Magazine* Vol. 124, No.1, October 1985

Dunn, Philippa, 'Spirit on the Scores' in *The StAndard* No. 17, November 2009

Hilles, Carolyn, 'A Haunted School Library where Mary, Queen of Scots Slept' in *Library Connection,* January 2004

Lambert, G.W., 'Scottish Haunts and Poltergeists: A Regional Study' in *Journal of the Society for Psychical Research* Volume 40, 1959-1960

Lamont-Brown, Raymond, 'The St Andrews Ghosthunter' in *Scotland's Magazine,* November 1975

———— 'Scottish Haunts and Poltergeists II' in *Journal of the Society for Psychical Research* Volume 42, 1963-1964

Lang, Andrew, 'At the Sign of the Ship' in *Longman's Magazine* Vol. 27, 1896

Matless, David, 'A geography of ghosts: the spectral landscapes of Mary Butts' in *Cultural Geographies* No. 15, 2008

Reid, Norman, ;The Skeleton of St Mary's' in *The StAndard* No. 13, March 2008

Rose, H.J., 'Scots Folklore Scraps' in *Folklore*, Vol. 43, No. 3, 1932

———— 'Ghost Summoning the Drowned' in *Folklore*, Vol. 55, No. 4 ,1944

Weldon, Fay, 'Dear William, Just a few things you should know about St Andrews' in *Daily Mail,* 18 August 2000

Newspapers

Aberdeen Weekly Journal: 1 & 9 February 1894

The Courier: 9, 10, 11, 13, 15, 20, 23 & 26 September 1958; 2 & 8 October 1958; 4 December 1967

Daily Mail: 8 April 1942

Daily Telegraph: 8 April 1942

Fife Herald & Journal: 27 January 1904

Fife Today: 24 October 2001

St Andrews Citizen: 8 February 1894; 24 September 1898; 25 May 1968

The Saturday Review of Politics, Literature, Science, and Art: January 1894

The Sun: 25 October 2000

Websites

The Sinner: www.thesinner.net

Index

If you enjoyed this book, you may also be interested in…

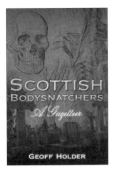

Scottish Bodysnatchers: A Gazetteer

GEOFF HOLDER

Grave robbing was a dark but profitable industry in pre-Victorian Scotland – criminals, gravediggers and middle-class medical students alike abstracted newly-buried corpses to send to the anatomy schools. Only after the trials of the infamous murderers Burke and Hare and the passing of the Anatomy Act of 1832 did the grisly trade end. Richly illustrated, filled with hundreds of stories of 'reanimated' corpses, daring thefts, black-hearted murders, this macabre guide will delight everyone who loves Scotland's dark past.

978 0 7524 5603 4

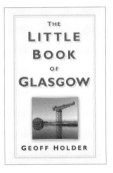

Haunted Dundee

GEOFF HOLDER

This chilling collection of true-life tales is teeming with terrifying hauntings from in and around Dundee. Featuring stories of unexplained phenomena, apparitions and poltergeists – including the tales of the White Ladies of Coffin Mill and Balgay Bridge, the hauntings of the historic ships Discovery and Unicorn, and a host of modern ghost sightings – this book is guaranteed to make your blood run cold.

978 0 7524 5849 6

The Little Book of Glasgow

GEOFF HOLDER

The Little Book of Glasgow is a funny, fast-paced, fact-packed compendium of the sort of frivolous, fantastic or simply strange information which no-one will want to be without. Here we find out about the most unusual crimes and punishments, eccentric inhabitants, famous sons and daughters and literally hundreds of wacky facts. Geoff Holder's book gathers together a myriad of data on Glasgow. A remarkably engaging little book, this is essential reading for visitors and locals alike.

978 0 7524 6004 8

Paranormal Perthshire

GEOFF HOLDER

Standing on a lonely Perthshire road is the only historic monument to a named witch in the whole of Britain. But did 'Maggie Wall' actually exist? This book reveals the controversial truth for the first time. (Even more surprising results come from a quest to uncover the reality of Perthshire's other famous witch, Kate McNiven.) With contemporary eye-witness accounts of ghosts, psychic episodes and encounters with supernatural beings, as well as more than fifty photographs, this book will delight all lovers of the mysterious and the paranormal.

978 0 7524 5421 4

Visit our website and discover thousands of other History Press books.

www.thehistorypress.co.uk